D0560301

The
Cavalier King
Charles Spaniel

An Owner's Guide To

A HAPPY HEALTHY PET

Howell Book House

IDG Books Worldwide, Inc.
An International Data Group Company
Foster City, CA • Chicago, IL • Indianapolis, IN • New York, NY

Howell Book House
IDG Books Worldwide, Inc.
An International Data Group Company
919 E. Hillsdale Boulevard, Suite 400
Foster City, CA 94404

For general information on IDG Books Worldwide's books in the U.S., please call our Consumer Customer Service department at 800-762-2974. For reseller information, including discounts and premium sales, please call our Reseller Customer Service department at 800-434-3422.

Library of Congress Cataloging-in-Publication Data
Moffat, Norma
The cavalier King Charles spaniel: an owner's guide to a happy healthy pet/Norma Moffat.
    p.cm
  Includes bibliographical references.
   1. Cavalier King Charles Spaniel I. Title
  ISBN 1-58245-125-7

Manufactured in the United States of America
10 9 8 7 6 5 4 3 2 1

Series Director: Susanna Thomas
Book Design: Michele Laseau
Cover Design: Iris Jeromnimon
External Features Illustration by Shelley Norris
Other Illustrations by Jeff Yesh
Photography:
  Front and back covers by Mary Bloom
  All photography by Mary Bloom unless otherwise noted.
    Joan Balzarini: 96
    Paulette Braun/Pets by Paulette: 96
    Buckinghambill American Cocker Spaniels: 148
    Sian Cox: 134
    Dr. Ian Dunbar: 98, 101, 103, 111, 116–117, 122, 123, 127
    Howell Book House: 24
    Dan Lyons: 96
    Norma Moffat: 12, 23, 25, 32, 55, 76
    Cathy Merrithew: 129
    Liz Palika: 133
    Susan Rezy: 96–97
    Judith Strom: 96, 107, 110, 128, 130, 135, 137, 139, 140, 144, 149, 150
Production Team: David Faust, Stephanie Lucas, and Heather Pope

Contents

Welcome
to the
World

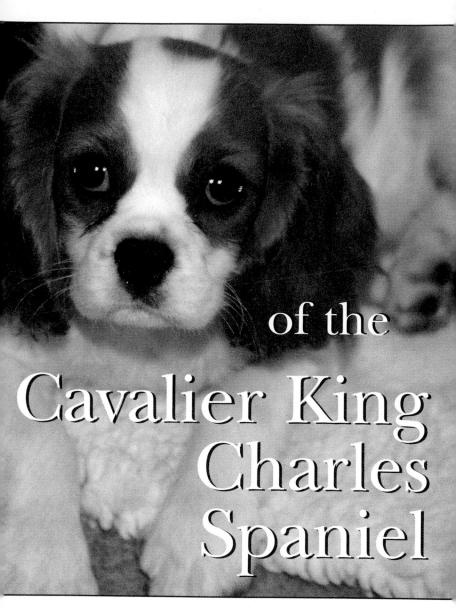

of the

Cavalier King
Charles
Spaniel

External Features of the Cavalier King Charles Spaniel

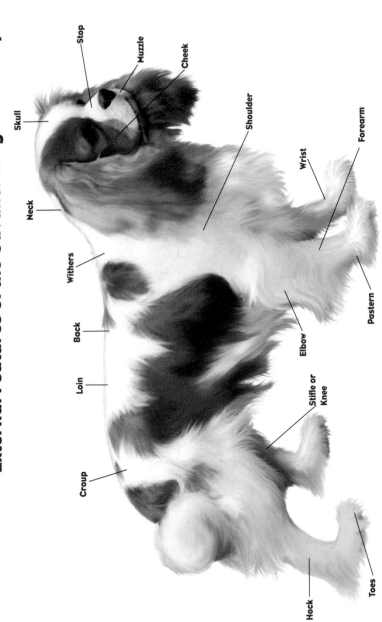

chapter 1

What Is a Cavalier King Charles Spaniel?

The Cavalier is a sporting toy spaniel with a sweet, affectionate nature that makes him ideal as a family pet. Happy to be with you no matter what your activity, the Cavalier will love to snuggle on your lap while you watch TV but will be equally enthusiastic about keeping you company on a hiking trail. The Cavalier has all the lively sporting instincts of his larger cousins, the Springer and the Cocker Spaniel, but contains them all in a small, portable package. This little spaniel is immensely adaptable to

5

an owner's lifestyle. He will be at home in the confines of the city or in the wide-open spaces of the country and he has but one requirement for his happiness: the companionship and love of a human family.

The Breed Standard

The breed was recognized by the American Kennel Club in 1997 only after the formation of the American Cavalier King Charles Spaniel Club. A Breed Standard was submitted and approved at that time. Every breed recognized by the American Kennel Club must have a Breed Standard, or a blueprint that describes the "perfect" dog. The following excerpt from the standard is a written description of the perfect Cavalier King Charles Spaniel. No such animal exists of course, but the aim of breeders is to try to produce that ideal specimen.

WHAT IS A BREED STANDARD?

A Breed Standard—a detailed description of an individual breed—is meant to portray the ideal specimen of that breed. This includes ideal structure, temperament, gait, type—all aspects of the dog. Because the Standard describes an ideal specimen, it isn't based on any particular dog. It is a concept against which judges compare actual dogs and breeders strive to produce dogs. At a dog show, the dog that wins is the one that comes closest, in the judges' opinion, to the Standard for its breed. Breed Standards are written by the breed parent clubs, the national organizations formed to oversee the well-being of the breed. They are voted on and approved by the members of the parent clubs.

Extracts from the AKC Standard for the CKCS

Below, extracts from the Cavalier King Charles Spaniel Breed Standard appear in italics. Explanations of the Standard's text appear in regular type.

GENERAL APPEARANCE

The Cavalier King Charles Spaniel is an active, graceful, well-balanced toy spaniel, very gay and free in action; fearless and sporting in character, yet at the same time gentle and affectionate. It is this typical gay temperament, combined with true elegance and royal appearance which are of paramount importance in the breed. Natural appearance with no trimming, sculpting or artificial alteration is essential to breed type. Note: The emphasis here is on a dog without any exaggerated features in size and shape, and a totally natural coat.

Size, Proportion, Substance

Size *Height 12 to 13 inches at the withers; weight proportionate to height, between 13 and 18 lbs. A small, well-balanced dog within these weights is desirable.*

Here is Ann's Son, the Cavalier on which the English Breed Standard was based.

Proportion *The body approaches squareness, yet if measured from point of shoulder to point of buttock, is slightly longer than the height at the withers.* Note: In ordinary language, the body is just slightly longer than its height. "Withers" refers to the highest point of the shoulder.

The Cavalier should have a natural appearance without trimming or sculpting.

Substance *Bone moderate in proportion to size. Weedy and coarse specimens are to be equally penalized.*

Head

Proportionate to size of dog, appearing neither too large nor too small for the body.

Expression *The sweet, gentle, melting expression is an important breed characteristic.*

Eyes *Large, round, but not prominent, and set well apart; color a warm, very dark brown, giving a lustrous, limpid look. Rims dark. There should be cushioning under the eyes which contributes to the soft expression. Faults—small, almond-shaped, prominent or light eyes; white surrounding ring.*

7

Welcome to
the World of
the Cavalier
King Charles
Spaniel

Ears *Set high, but not close, on top of the head. Leather long with plenty of feathering and wide enough so that when the dog is alert, the ears fan slightly forward to frame the face.*

Skull *Slightly rounded, but without dome or peak; it should appear flat because of the high placement of the ears. Stop is moderate, neither filled nor deep.*

Muzzle *Full muzzle slightly tapered. Length from base of stop to tip of nose about 1¹/₂ inches. Face well filled below eyes.* Note: "Well filled" refers to the plushy cushions underneath the eyes and on the muzzle. In sum, it is the beautiful head with its essentially sweet expression and soulful eyes that best expresses the character of this breed.

NECK, TOPLINE AND BODY

Neck *Fairly long, without throatiness, well enough muscled to form a slight arch at the crest. Set smoothly into nicely sloping shoulders to give an elegant look.*

Topline *Level both when moving and standing. Body—Short-coupled with ribs well sprung but not barreled.* Note: "Short-coupled" refers to the length of the body from front to back legs. A square, rather than a rectangular body is desirable. Chest moderately deep, extending to elbows allowing ample heart room. Slightly less body at the flank than at the last rib, but with no tucked-up appearance.

Tail *Well set on, carried happily but never much above the level of the back, and in constant characteristic motion when the dog is in action. Docking is optional. If docked, no more than one third to be removed.* Note: "Docking" refers

THE AMERICAN KENNEL CLUB

Familiarly referred to as "the AKC," the American Kennel Club is a nonprofit organization devoted to the advancement of purebred dogs. The AKC maintains a registry of recognized breeds and adopts and enforces rules for dog events including shows, obedience trials, field trials, hunting tests, lure coursing, herding, earthdog trials, agility and the Canine Good Citizen program. It is a club of clubs, established in 1884 and composed, today, of more than 500 autonomous dog clubs throughout the United States. Each club is represented by a delegate; the delegates make up the legislative body of the AKC, voting on rules and electing directors. The American Kennel Club maintains the Stud Book, the record of every dog ever registered with the AKC, and publishes a variety of materials on purebred dogs, including a monthly magazine, books and numerous educational pamphlets. For more information, contact the AKC at the address listed in Chapter 13, "Resources," and look for the names of their publications in Chapter 12, "Recommended Reading."

to cutting off the end of the tail to give a balanced look to the dog. In England, the country of origin, docking is now prohibited by law.

COAT

Of moderate length, silky, free from curl. Slight wave permissible. Feathering on ears, chest, legs and tail should be long and feathering on the feet is a feature of the breed. No trimming of the dog is permitted. Specimens where the coat has been altered by trimming, clipping, or by artificial means shall be so severely penalized as to be effectively eliminated from competition. Hair growing between the pads on the underside of the feet may be trimmed. Note: This is the only Spaniel breed in which the feathers on the feet or "bedroom slippers" are left long and untrimmed. The emphasis once again is on the natural appearance of the dog.

The Cavalier's eyes should be large and round and give him a lustrous, limpid look.

COLOR

Blenheim   *Rich chestnut markings well broken up on a clear, pearly white ground. The ears must be chestnut and the color evenly spaced on the head and surrounding both eyes, with a white blaze between the eyes and ears, in the center of which may be the "lozenge" or Blenheim spot. The lozenge is a unique and desirable, though not essential, characteristic of the Blenheim.*

Tricolor   *Jet black markings well broken up on a clear, pearly white ground. The ears must be black and the color evenly spaced on the head and surrounding both eyes, with a white blaze between the eyes. Rich tan markings over the eyes, on cheeks, inside ears and on underside of tail.*

Ruby   *Whole rich colored red.*

Black and Tan   *Jet black with rich, bright tan markings over eyes, on cheeks, inside ears, on chest, legs and underside of tail.*

Faults *Heavy ticking on Blenheims or Tricolors, white marks on Rubies or Black and Tans.* Note: Blenheims and tricolors are also referred to as "particolors" because of the white in the coat, while rubies and black and tans are referred to as "wholecolors" because of the lack of white. The marking faults referred to are significant for the breeder, but should be of no importance to a person considering a Cavalier as a pet.

GAIT

The Blenheim colored dog (left). Notice the white blaze between the eyes and ears.

A tricolor Cavalier puppy (right).

Free moving and elegant in action, with good reach in front and sound, driving rear action. When viewed from the side the movement exhibits a good length of stride, and viewed from the front it is straight and true. Note: The lovely flowing stride of a properly structured Cavalier emphasizes its relationship to the larger sporting spaniels and its origin as a hunting bird dog.

TEMPERAMENT

Gay, friendly, non-aggressive, with no tendency towards nervousness or shyness. Bad temper, shyness and meanness are not to be tolerated and are to be so severely penalized as to effectively remove the specimen from competition.

The AKC Breed Standard gives a mental picture of perfect Cavalier conformation, and it is this picture which all serious breeders will endeavor to bring to life in their stock. For a person considering the purchase of a Cavalier as a pet, the two main concerns should be temperament and good health. To the eye of the average person, every Cavalier is attractive, and the small imperfections that cause a breeder to let a puppy go as a pet cannot be seen by the pet owner. The temperament of the Cavalier should be as sweet and charming as his appearance. He will bark when someone comes to the door, but once a visitor is inside, that person is assumed to be a friend and will receive an enthusiastic welcome. For hundreds of years this breed's function has been loving companionship to the human, and this is the greatest gift the Cavalier has to bestow.

The ruby (left) is a solid colored dog with a rich, whole red.

A black and tan Cavalier (right) out for sunbathing.

chapter 2

The Cavalier's Ancestry

(photo by Norma Moffat)

There has been much speculation about the origin of the Cavalier King Charles Spaniel as we know it today. It is possible that the Cavalier developed from a red and white dog indigenous to Malta or Italy that was crossed with a spaniel-type dog from the Far East in the thirteenth century. Another popular theory is that all spaniels, as their name implies, originated in Spain. It is a fact, however, that the toy spaniel was refined as a breed in England, and there is no doubt that there were inclusions of sporting spaniel types in the bloodlines, too. From the beginning the Cavalier has had a dual purpose as both a pet and a sporting companion in the field.

Whatever its origin, it is plain that the Cavalier is a descendant of the "Spaniel Gentle" dogs seen in so many pictures of English lords and ladies from the sixteenth century onwards. There are two charming paintings of the children of King Charles I from about 1630 by Anthony van Dyck. In one, a Blenheim may be seen on the right-hand side of the children, and in the other, there are two keeping the children company. Many of the spaniels depicted from this period look finer in bone than the Cavaliers of today, and have longer, rather pointed noses, but the fact that they are included in so many antique pictures of royalty and nobility tells us that the toy spaniel has been kept as a beloved pet and valued for its beauty and personality for hundreds of years.

The Cavalier at Court

The first recorded royal person who had a beloved toy spaniel was Mary Queen of Scots, and we know this because of a written record of the manner of her death. This ill-fated member of the royal family was beheaded on the order of Queen Elizabeth I in 1587. It was reported that a little spaniel walked close under her voluminous skirts to the scaffold and emerged after Mary was dealt her deathblow. The dog would not leave her body until someone picked him up and took him away. He died two days later and was said to have pined away from grief.

Mary Queen of Scots was not the only Royal to have a toy spaniel that was faithful unto death. Charles I also met the executioner's ax after the civil war between the republican roundheads and royalist Cavaliers in 1649. It is said that he walked to the place of his execution with his black and white toy spaniel named Rogue at his side. After the execution, one of the Roundheads took Rogue and put him on display in London.

Though kings, queen, lords and ladies all treasured their toy spaniels, it was after the demise of the republic and in the restored reign of Charles II that the breed became famous throughout the land as the king had a large number of the little dogs that were allowed to follow him wherever he went. Charles II was known as the Cavalier King, and his first parliament as the Cavalier Parliament.

When a name came to be chosen for the breed in 1925 to distinguish it from the flat-faced toy spaniel, it seemed logical to call it by the name of the Cavalier

King, Charles II, who first brought it to prominence in England. This king was so fond of his pack of little dogs that, according to famous diarist Samuel Pepys, he neglected the business of the kingdom to play with them. A member of the court, complaining about the general doggy disorder in the royal apartments, declared that the king "took delight in having a number of little spaniels follow him and lie in his bedchamber, where he suffered the bitches to puppy, which rendered it very offensive and indeed the whole court nasty and stinking." In this case, the king's love for his dogs was not only blind, but had no sense of smell!

Cavaliers have dined with kings and queens. Here, two Cavaliers await tea service (or is that T-bone service?).

Charles II died a natural death in his own bed, and was succeeded by his brother James II, who also succumbed to the charm of the toy spaniel. James had occasion to take a sea voyage, and his dogs accompanied him on the ship. A very bad storm blew up and it seemed as though they were on the point of abandoning ship. James was heard to cry, "Save the dogs and the Duke of Monmouth!" It seems in this case that the toy spaniels had as much importance in the king's mind as his own son. While this attitude seems somewhat extreme, it is an example of the close emotional bond that king and commoner alike have with this most charming of breeds.

Signs of Things to Come

The long-nosed toy spaniel of King Charles's day went out of fashion during the reign of King William of Orange and Queen Mary when they brought from Holland a number of dogs from their favorite breed, the Pug. Perhaps there was some interbreeding between spaniels and Pugs, but in any case, there resulted a toy spaniel with a domed head and flat undershot muzzle. This short-muzzled dog was named the King Charles Spaniel, and became the type on display at early British shows and at the famous Crufts Show in London. In North America today, this breed is known as the English Toy Spaniel. Breeders of these dogs would occasionally find a long-muzzled puppy in a litter and this would either be put out of the breeding program or sold as a pet.

In the late eighteenth century, John Duke of Marlborough had a pack of red and white toy spaniels that he used for hunting. They were hardy little dogs and the duke recorded that they were well able to keep up with a trotting horse. His estate was named Blenheim Castle in honor of his victorious battle at that German town, and that is why this color of spaniel became known as Blenheim.

There is a legend concerning the duke's wife, Sarah, which illustrates the empathy between owner and dog. While the duke was at the battle of Blenheim the duchess was waiting anxiously for news of the battle, whether of victory or defeat. On her lap was a little pregnant spaniel on whose head the duchess pressed her thumb while stroking her. When the puppies were born, all bore a chestnut-colored imprint of the duchess's thumb, and this is supposed to be the origin of the lozenge or thumbprint mark to be found only on the head of the perfectly marked Blenheim.

In the Victorian era, toy spaniels once more came into the public eye because of the Queen's beloved tricolor pet named Dash. Interestingly enough, Dash was not one of the more popular short-nosed spaniels, but is recognizable in the portraits painted of him as being very like the modern Cavalier. On the very day in 1837 that Victoria was crowned, she recorded in her diary that she came home from this momentous event, changed her clothes and gave Dash a bath.

There are many pictures in oils and in needlework of Dash. One of the most interesting paintings is by Sir Edwin Landseer, the artist who also designed the lions in London's Trafalgar Square. It shows Dash lying in luxury on a velvet cushion surrounded by other pets of the royal household, a parrot, a deerhound and a greyhound. One of the rarer representations of Dash is an Irish Belleek porcelain figure of him lying on a cushion with the queen's fan between his paws.

Queen Victoria had a tricolor named Dash who looked very similar to the Cavaliers we keep as pets today. Here, a modern tricolor enjoys this ride on a swing.

When Dash died, the queen herself wrote the epitaph for his tombstone: *Here lies Dash, the favorite spaniel of Her Majesty Queen Victoria, by whose command this memorial was erected. He died on the 20th December 1840 in his ninth year. His attachment was without selfishness, his playfulness without malice, his fidelity without deceit. Reader, if you would live beloved and die regretted, profit by the example of Dash.*

The artist Sir Edwin Landseer produced other portraits of toy spaniels, and one that all breeders have in their homes is known as either *Waiting for the Master* or *The Cavalier's Pets*. It depicts the large-brimmed hat complete with long curled feather typical of that worn by a Cavalier gentleman. In front of the hat is a pair of elegant leather gauntlets. On one side of the hat is a pretty little Blenheim that has a perfect lozenge and on the other a sweet-faced tricolor. They are lying snuggled up close to the hat, their heads are down on their paws and they wait in perfect confidence that the master will return. The picture has a touching quality and it illustrates clearly the Cavalier's trust in and devotion to its owner. The original of this picture is in the Tate Gallery in London, England, and prints may still occasionally be found in framing galleries and art shops in this country.

In 1987 the Royal Doulton China Company released a limited edition statue of Queen Victoria with two Blenheim Cavaliers. This is not a representation of the stern old dowager queen in her widow's cap and black dress, but shows a very young, rather pretty woman dressed in a simple pink gown. One Cavalier is held in the crook of her arm, and she is bending to caress the head of another as it looks up at her. This is how we can imagine the 18-year-old queen on the day of her coronation, relaxing after the rigors of the day by playing with her pets.

It was due to the queen's interest in the toy spaniel that pottery dogs, known as "Staffordshires" because of the location of the pottery factories in England, became the rage with the British public. These pottery dogs were made from the late 1850s until the 1930s. They were always in facing pairs to represent a male and female, and they are easily recognizable as Cavaliers. What makes them so charming is that they are often painted and glazed in bright fanciful colors. Throughout England, the homes of the working class soon displayed Staffordshire dogs, which were usually placed one at each side of the fireplace. Since they are quite fragile, only a fraction of them survive intact to the present day. These pottery dogs are rare, highly collectible antiques and in this country a pair in good condition would be worth $1,000 or more. I have collected a number of them and my most treasured pair are black with gold accents. I purchased them in England many years ago for the bargain price of $80. To my delight, they have recently been valued at $1,200.

The Better to Smell You With

After the reign of Victoria, the short-nosed variety of the toy spaniel was still the most common. The reappearance of the original type of toy spaniel, the Cavalier, must be credited to Mr. Roswell Eldridge, an American who went to England in the early 1920s to purchase a breeding pair of the "old nosey type" as seen in the pictures of England's noble families. He could not find them, and so offered prizes at the most famous of British dog shows known as "Crufts" from 1926 to 1931 for "Blenheim Spaniels of the Old Type, as shown in the pictures of Charles II's time, long face, no stop, flat skull not inclined to be domed, with spot in centre of skull." There was a renewed interest by a small group of dedicated English breeders, led by Mrs. Amice Pitt, in producing the old type of toy spaniel, and the Cavalier King Charles Spaniel Club was formed in 1928.

*Portraits and
other art depict-
ing Cavaliers
have been popu-
lar for decades
and remain so.*

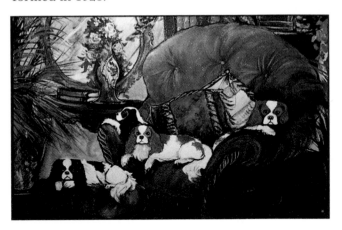

There were not many Cavaliers, or the "old nosey type," left in England, and this situation resulted in a fair amount of close linebreeding and inbreeding by those interested in restoring the original toy spaniel as a breed. There are also stories from this era, though no one seems to be able to prove or disprove them, that the Papillon and the Shetland Sheepdog were crossed judiciously with toy spaniels in some breeding programs of this era to bring back the "old nosey type." If in fact these stories have some foundation, all we can say is that these breeders were successful in their efforts.

Hard times were in view for the Cavalier and for all purebreds in England with the advent of the Second World War in 1939. There was food rationing, and hardly enough food to keep the human population healthy. Many kennels stopped their breeding programs entirely until the war was over, and the numbers of toy spaniels declined quite drastically. After the war, Mrs. Amice Pitt and her small, dedicated group of breeders began once more to try to establish lines of the longer nosed toy spaniels that we know as Cavaliers today. The dog that was to be most influential in re-establishing the ancient breed was Ann's Son owned by Miss Mostyn Walker, and the original English Breed Standard was based on his conformation. A written description of Ann's Son by Mrs. Massingham, a well-known breeder, exudes respect for this dog:

Pillows are another popular decoration depicting Cavaliers.

A toy spaniel of thirteen pounds, short in the back, entirely flat head, streaming ears to his legs, large dark eyes wide apart, nose long, tipped with jet to match his dark eyes, a white blaze running right up the forehead, thick soft silky coat marked with red and silver blenheim, and sound as a bell. He was supreme. I realise that it is not only all the perfect points that gave him glory, it was the overall quality which this exquisite little dog had and which shone out of his face that made him Best Ever Born.

What's in a Name?

Until 1945 all toy spaniels, whether short or long faced, were known as King Charles Spaniels, but once there were a number of the long-faced types in the championship ring, their breeders applied to register them separately. Three ladies, Mrs. Pitt, Mrs. Eldred and Mme Harper Trois-Fontaines, studied the English Kennel Club registrations to determine which dogs should become part of a separate registration for the long-nosed variety of toy spaniel. They compiled a list of dogs from which all Cavaliers of today are descended. Of these three pioneers in re-creating the breed, one is still living and breeding Cavaliers under the kennel name of Turnworth. She is Mrs. Katie Eldred, whose home is in the Vancouver area of British Columbia, Canada. Separate registration was granted in 1945 and the name Cavalier King Charles was chosen in honor of the king who was so famous for his "pack of little dogs."

Cavaliers are still popular in England with royals, the aristocracy and those high in government. Princess Margaret, sister of Queen Elizabeth II, treasured one called Rowley who was her companion for many years. Despite her royal history, it does not matter to this most affectionate of dogs whether you are king or commoner, rich or poor, all that matters is that she has someone to love and to be loved by in return. Cavaliers have become one of the most popular toy breeds in England and may be seen everywhere in town and country, trotting happily along with their owners.

Many celebrities have loved a Cavalier over the years and it's not difficult to see why.

The Cavalier Comes to America

The American history of the Cavalier begins with Mrs. W. Lyons Brown of the Sutherland estate in Prospect, Kentucky, who brought a dog home from England in 1956. With the help of Elizabeth Spalding of Maine, one of the early importers of Cavaliers, and a group of breed enthusiasts, she founded the Cavalier King Charles Spaniel Club USA, which maintained its own Stud Book and held specialty shows for Cavaliers only. This club continues and flourishes to the present day.

In England, the country of origin of the breed, and in all other countries except the USA, Cavaliers have always been part of a national registry. In 1994, the American Cavalier King Charles Spaniel Club was founded by a group of experienced breeders who wished to apply for AKC recognition and registration for Cavaliers. The ACKCSC became the AKC parent club of the breed, and today Cavaliers may be seen in the showring throughout the country.

FAMOUS OWNERS OF CAVALIER KING CHARLES SPANIELS

King Charles I

Mary Queen of Scots

Diane Sawyer

Sylvester Stallone

Frank Sinatra

Nancy Reagan

There are many celebrities in America who have owned and loved Cavaliers including Sylvester Stallone, Frank Sinatra and Nancy Reagan. Mrs. Reagan obtained her Cavalier through her friend Pat Buckley who had two Cavaliers bought from Irene Murphy, a well-known breeder. There is a story that when Pat Buckley mentioned to this breeder that she had a famous friend, whose name could not be revealed, who would like to have a Cavalier puppy, Irene replied that unless she could meet the person and approve of her, no puppy would be forthcoming. It is a credit to Irene Murphy that she was so caring about her puppy that she would not place it unless she knew exactly where and to whom it was going.

Diane Sawyer, television host of *Good Morning America*, and her husband, playwright and producer Mike Nichols, are the latest people in the public eye to own and love a Cavalier King Charles Spaniel. I am happy to say that their tricolor female is one of my own breeding. Brinklow La Bamba Lila is her registered name, and to date, Lila has made two appearances on *Good Morning America* with her doting owner.

chapter 3

The World According to the Cavalier King Charles Spaniel

The world of the Cavalier is essentially your world, since this little dog is the companion par excellence of dog breeds, eager to please and adaptable to any lifestyle. From morning until night, as long as you are home, your Cavalier will be gazing at you with those big soft eyes and will follow you all day no matterwhat your activity. If you like to start the day with a run or a brisk walk, your Cavalier will keep pace with you. If you live in an urban area and your walks are around city blocks, be warned that your Cavalier must be kept on a lead for his own safety, even if you have taken him to obedience classes and he generally stays near you. Any dog can be easily distracted and run heedlessly across a road to chase a squirrel or greet another dog even if there are two lines of traffic zooming down the road.

In a city park, he needs to be on a long line or retractable lead so that you have control. Being a sociable sort, he may want to greet every other dog he sees, not realizing that some breeds can be aggressive or protective of their owners. Since he is much smaller than most of the dogs you will encounter, it is simple to reel him in at any sign of danger. In order to give your Cavalier the exercise he needs and keep him in good condition, you should walk so that he must trot to keep up with you.

Hunting Instincts

If you are in a place where he can be taken safely off lead, you will notice, though he runs free, he will keep an eye on you to be sure you are within reach. Given a large grassy open area the Cavalier will naturally "quarter" the field, running diagonally back and forth with his nose low to the ground. His hunting instincts are in full play as he picks up the hundreds of scents wafting upwards.

We have one small but mighty black and tan female called Polka who displays the breed's hunting instincts by being a great butterfly chaser. She knows they are found in the long grass, and though we cannot see her progress because the grass is taller than she is, there is the occasional sighting of a sleek black head and a pair of flying ears as she bounds upward like a butterfly-seeking missile. To my knowledge, she has never succeeded in catching her quarry, but it is the game that is the fun, and we get as much pleasure from watching as she does from the chase.

Cavaliers will retrieve, even if it means getting wet! (photo by Norma Moffat)

The Retrieving Cavalier

The Cavalier also confirms his sporting origin by being a very good retriever if encouraged early. Of our ten dogs, five are natural retrievers, bringing back a ball or catching a Frisbee with great enthusiasm. My 3-year-old

Blenheim girl, Joy, is amazingly skillful not only in her ability to retrieve on the fly and bring a ball to hand, but to find one that other dogs have lost in deep grass or bush. If a dog has lost a ball, and I have some idea of its vicinity, I point to the area and give Joy the command "find it." She will search that patch of ground over and over until I tell her to stop. Very often she finds the ball in a short time and comes trotting over proudly, tail held high and eyes sparkling, to present it and be told how very clever she is.

Though a Cavalier running free seems to be independent, you will notice that he keeps one eye open for your whereabouts. If you suddenly change direction, he will do likewise to retain that link with you. To be happy, he must have human company most of the time, unlike the terriers, for instance, who were bred as outdoor dogs and independent workers.

CHARACTERISTICS OF THE CAVALIER KING CHARLES SPANIEL

Gentle

Sweet

Loyal

Eager to please

Adaptable

Sensitive

Loveable lap dog

The Sturdy Cavalier

Though he is a true toy in size, the Cavalier is a sturdy dog and well able to keep up a trotting pace for a number of miles. My husband, at 72 years of age, is a great walker, and has taken part in many long, charity-sponsored hikes. He likes to take two or three of the dogs with him, and he declares that they are much livelier at the end of the walk than he is. One benefit of being out in public with a Cavalier is that you will meet people and make new friends as people stop to ask what the breed is and "Can I please pet your dog?" It does not matter how many times this happens, the Cavalier is the epitome of trust and will greet anyone with a gently wagging tail.

The Water Dog

If you spend part of the summer in a location where there is access to water, a freshwater lake or by the seashore, you will soon discover that your Cavalier, like other spaniels, is a real water dog. The first sight of an expanse of water causes great excitement. Your Cavalier will tiptoe in and stand there for a while. Then a genetic light in his brain seems to switch on and away he goes, swimming as though he has done it all his life.

I brought Daphne, my 5-month-old tricolor puppy, up to our summer home on a lake for the first time in July of this year. She didn't know what to make of the water at first and stood on the shore barking, telling me how foolish I was to be paddling in the shallows. Then I teased her with a ball and threw it just a few inches into the water. She pounced with glee, causing great splashing. Then I threw the ball a little further. In no time, Daphne was swimming and retrieving like a veteran. After a few days, Daphne would run down to the water by herself early in the morning while the lake was misty and placid, and take a long leisurely swim just for the fun of it.

Cavaliers are definitely not afraid of the water! But be careful to dry them thoroughly after a swim, especially inside the ears where problems can develop. (photo by Norma Moffat)

One word of caution about the ears is necessary here. Adult Cavalier ears are very hairy, even on the inside. It is essential to keep them dry to avoid problems such as canker or other bacterial infection. The easiest way to deal with this is to dry the ear with a towel to get rid of the excess moisture, lift the ear and use a hair dryer on a "cool and low" setting to dry the inside gently and thoroughly.

The Cavalier Stretch

After your morning walk at breakfast time you must resist the urge to give your Cavalier treats from the table. It is so hard to resist those begging eyes, but the Cavalier is prone to put on weight easily and this applies particularly to females. A small, good quality dog biscuit first thing in the morning is all that is needed to keep your dog going until his daily meal, which should be fed in the late afternoon or early evening.

Perhaps you like to sit and read the morning paper after breakfast. Your Cavalier will come to you and perform what I call the "Cavalier Stretch." He will put his two front feet on your thigh and stretch his whole body and head upward as a sign of affection. This is a definite breed trait, which even young puppies will display. Then you can pet him a little, or give way completely and invite him onto your lap. In olden times of travel by horse and carriage, a lady would take the cozy body of a little spaniel on her lap to help keep herself warm during a winter trip. Thus, the nickname of the toy spaniel in those days was the "Spaniel Gentle" or "Comforter," a dog considered pretty enough and civilized enough to be a constant companion for any lord or lady.

The Cavalier Needs You

The Cavalier is so pliable by nature that he will tolerate being left for a few hours while everyone is away from home, but he suffers if separated from his family for too long. He needs human company more than any other breed of dog, and will become depressed if left alone for long periods of time, either inside or outside the house.

The All-Weather Cavalier

I am often asked if the Cavalier needs a jacket or sweater to keep warm in the winters of the middle and northern part of the country. It is true that because dogs live in centrally heated houses, they do not grow thick coats for the winter. In general, the Cavalier does not need to be dressed to go out even in the coldest weather, as long as he is being active. Leaving him out in the yard by himself on a very cold day is a sure way to give him a chill, but as long as he is walking with you, or generally keeping on the move, his activity will keep him warm enough.

In southern climates, you may need to have your Cavalier clipped to keep him comfortable on hot days. Once a Cavalier has been spayed or neutered, and the hormones are no longer working as they once were, there will be accelerated coat growth. The texture will change from relatively short and silky to long, thick and rather woolly, and the dog will need to be taken to a groomer on a regular basis.

Snoring and Snorting

Once your Cavalier has had his morning walk and social time with you, he will happily settle down to nap for an hour or two at your feet. The occasional Cavalier turns out to be a snorer. The culprits seem to be those individuals that have shorter than average noses. We have a ruby girl named Dina, now 9 years old, who has a deep reverberating snore worthy of a Labrador Retriever. At first, the noise was bothersome, but now we are so accustomed to it we consider it a lullaby. In any case, we don't think the snoring is a serious enough problem to deny her bed privileges.

There is another minor behavior associated with the structure of soft palate and uvula, called snorting, and this usually happens when the dog is excited. To the uninitiated, it seems as though the dog is gasping for air as he makes loud snorting noises with his mouth wide open. There is no danger to the dog, and the behavior will subside on its own with no ill effects. You can, however, stop the snorting almost immediately by holding the dog's mouth shut and placing a finger over the nostrils to cut off the air temporarily. Sometimes I forget to tell new puppy owners of this behavior, and I get a panic phone call to the effect that there is something seriously wrong with the puppy's breathing. I am happy to reassure them that there is nothing wrong, and to describe the remedy.

Cavaliers are adorable when they nap, but they are prone to snoring.

A Happy Car Passenger

If your day includes a trip in the car, the Cavalier will enjoy it thoroughly as he is an excellent traveler and does not get carsick. He will want to sit in the front passenger seat so that he can be near you. I always advise people to crate the dog for safety's sake when traveling, but it does take some enjoyment away from him, as he cannot gaze out of the window at the passing scene. A good compromise is to get a dog harness, which attaches to the safety belt. This can be obtained at any large pet-supply store.

Gentle Discipline Is Needed

Dinnertime is a highlight of the Cavalier day and a time when he will get excited and tend to bark and jump up on you and anyone else in the vicinity. Teach him when he is very young to sit and wait for his food or for any treat. It is easy to spoil such a sweet and lovable dog, but a Cavalier needs discipline just like any other breed, or he will become demanding and not a pleasure to live with. Having said that, I must emphasize that the very soft nature of this breed means that only incentive and reward training should be used. Any physical punishment can ruin the temperament of the Cavalier and make him shy. There is nothing more upsetting to see than a Cavalier who creeps away when company comes, when he should be moving forward with ever-wagging tail to greet a visitor.

You and your Cavalier will benefit from reward-based training.

A Burglar's Friend

There is no guard instinct in the Cavalier. Though he will bark when someone comes to the door, it is bark of excitement rather than warning. He will greet any visitor with enthusiasm, and I believe that he will welcome a burglar as long as that burglar made a fuss of him.

Scooting

Talking of visitors, the Cavalier has one habit that is rather disconcerting, particularly when you consider how sweet and pretty the breed is. You have a house full of company and wish them to meet your little canine treasure. In comes your elegant, aristocratic Cavalier and begins to scoot his bottom along your best oriental carpet, rear legs held high in the air, a rather disgusting demonstration. No, he does not have worms or impacted anal glands; this is a breed trait that starts in puppyhood, and one we have learned to live with. All you can do is to distract the dog to stop his performance, and this is easily done by a quiet word. He will soon remember his manners and work his charm on a roomful of people, going from one to the other to give a greeting and get a pat in return.

Your Bed Is My Bed

At the end of the day, the Cavalier is totally convinced that your bed is where he belongs. When a puppy leaves my house, I tell the new owners to start as they mean to go on, and if they wish their dog to sleep in his own crate or bed, then that must be done from the first night onwards. Nine times out of ten I will get a phone call during which the new owner will say something like this: "We took the crate into our bedroom and put him in it, but he whined and cried and his eyes looked so sad we couldn't stand it. As soon as we put him up on the foot of the bed he settled right down and we didn't hear a peep out of him all night." A Cavalier makes an excellent bed dog and fits his silky body perfectly into the bend of your knee. The only problem is that he may suffer occasionally from a desire to express an excess of

---

A DOG'S SENSES

Sight: With their eyes located farther apart than ours, dogs can detect movement at a greater distance than we can, but they can't see as well up close. They can also see better in less light, but can't distinguish many colors.

Sound: Dogs can hear about four times better than we can, and they can hear high-pitched sounds especially well. Their ancestors, the wolves, howled to let other wolves know where they were; our dogs do the same, but they have a wider range of vocalizations, including barks, whimpers, moans and whines.

Smell: A dog's nose is his greatest sensory organ. His sense of smell is so great he can follow a trail that's weeks old, detect odors diluted to one-millionth the concentration we'd need to notice them, even sniff out a person under water!

Taste: Dogs have fewer taste buds than we do, so they're likelier to try anything—and usually do, which is why it's especially important for their owners to monitor their food intake. Dogs are omnivores, which means they eat meat as well as vegetable matter like grasses and weeds.

Touch: Dogs are social animals and love to be petted, groomed and played with.

affection in the middle of the night. He will creep up the bed and press himself against your mouth and nose, cutting off your air supply. Your dreams may be suddenly filled with a sensation of suffocation and you wake with a start to find little precious showing you how much he loves you. This is a small price to pay for a companion whose uncritical affection, merry disposition and charming ways make your life happier.

Therapy and Helper Dog

Cavaliers make excellent pet therapy dogs. They can be taken into seniors' homes and hospitals and are small enough to be placed on laps where they love to

be. Even people with Alzheimer's disease will recognize an affectionate small dog and will pet it when they have otherwise been uncommunicative for a long time. Some Cavaliers have also been trained as helper dogs for the deaf. They

No matter your lifestyle, your Cavalier will fit in perfectly.

are temperamentally stable and intelligent enough and the right size to jump on the deaf person when the doorbell or the telephone rings, and then take them to the object that is making the noise.

Cavalier to the Rescue

The devotion of the Cavalier to his family, along with his remarkable intelligence, is exemplified by a dog I placed in a pet home whose call name is Charlie. It is always surprising to a breeder when a pet owner selects this name for a Cavalier, since it is part of the name of the breed, but it happens quite often.

When Charlie was about 2 years old, I received a remarkable telephone call from the owner to tell me, "My mother says that Charlie saved her life!" The woman and her daughter had taken Charlie with them when they went to stay with an elderly grandmother for the summer. She had a pretty property near a river in the country. Charlie was left with grandmother and her helper while mother and daughter went away for a few days. Late one night, Charlie and the grandmother went out for a little walk by the river. It had been raining and the steep bank of the river was slippery. The elderly lady fell down the bank into the very cold, deep river and could not pull herself out, though she managed to cling to the bottom of the bank.

Charlie ran back to the house and set up a frantic barking outside the sleeping helper's window. This woman woke with the noise and when it continued, she went outside to see why Charlie was making such a fuss. As soon as Charlie saw her he began to run towards the river barking frantically, then back to the woman, repeating this maneuver until she followed him. She found the old lady and was not strong enough to pull her out, but she ran for help to a nearby house. When she came back with help, Charlie was at the bottom of the bank licking the old lady's face as though making an effort to keep her conscious. At least this was the interpretation Charlie's owner put on his actions. The grandmother was hypothermic and stressed, but after a few hours was none the worse for her accident. Charlie had been treasured before this incident, but you can be sure that from that day forward he was thought to be near human and treated accordingly.

The Cavalier and Children

Though the Cavalier is perfectly adapted to living with older people, he adjusts well to all other ages, too. One of the questions I am frequently asked is whether this breed is a good one to have when there are children in the family. The answer is a qualified yes, depending upon the children, because the average Cavalier is so affectionate and forgiving of the slightly rough treatment that can be handed out by children.

A puppy usually goes to its new home at the age of 8 weeks when it is between 3 and 5 pounds in weight. If there are toddlers or small children in the family, they must be supervised when playing with the puppy, and they must never be allowed to pick the puppy up and walk around with it. I have seen a few disasters as a puppy wriggles and jumps out of a child's arms and is injured in the fall. The floor is the perfect place for child and puppy to be together as it is safer and less intimidating for the puppy to have someone at his own level.

I always ask a family to visit if they are interested in purchasing a puppy, and the reason is that I wish to meet the children to assess their behavior with the dogs before I will consider the family suitable. Children who pay attention to instruction on how to approach the dogs, and who are gentle with them, will usually treat a puppy with respect. Little horrors who grab at the dogs, and run around making loud noises with no discipline from the parents, will probably end up making a puppy nervous.

Temperaments of some puppies are more suited to children than others. All ranges of temperament in the Cavalier should be sweet and loving, but they vary just as temperaments do in a human family. The extroverted, confident puppy will be happy with the noise and activity generated by a house full of children, while this situation would be intimidating for the quiet, submissive puppy who would be better suited to a home of adults only.

The Cavalier is affectionate towards and tolerant of children. (photo by Norma Moffat)

The average size of Cavalier litter is only three puppies (though there can be more), and by the age of 7 to 8 weeks differences in temperament will be obvious to the breeder. Therefore I believe that the breeder is best qualified to decide which family should have which puppy. When I tell prospective puppy purchasers that this is my policy, they are disappointed at first since they wish to choose their own puppy. When I explain the reasoning, however, most people agree to abide by my decision. Given that a puppy has a stable temperament and has been well socialized before leaving its littermates, it will adapt to almost any family. I tell them when they come to pick up their puppy that they have a baby who will pick up all his lasting habits in the next eight to ten weeks, and that they should pay particular attention to the emotional welfare and training of the puppy in this most important period.

More Information on the Cavalier King Charles Spaniel

CLUBS

The Cavalier King Charles Spaniel Club, USA
www.ckcsc.org

The Lucky Star Fund (Rescue Organization)
www.kantucavaliers.com/kantu/luckystar/

MAGAZINES

Cavalier Crossroads, The Online Magazine for Cavalier Fanciers
www.ckcs.com

The Royal Spaniels (a quarterly periodical)
Publisher/Editor Michael Allen
14531 Jefferson Street
Midway City, CA 92655-1030

BOOKS

Here are three excellent reference books by respected English breeders and judges:

Evans, John. *Cavalier King Charles Spaniels.* New York: Howell Book House, 1990.

Field, Bruce. *The Cavalier King Charles Spaniel,* revised edition. Clerkenwell Green, London: Robert Hale Limited, Clerkenwell House, 1996.

Smith, Sheila. *Cavalier King Charles Spaniels Today.* New York: Howell Book House, 1995.

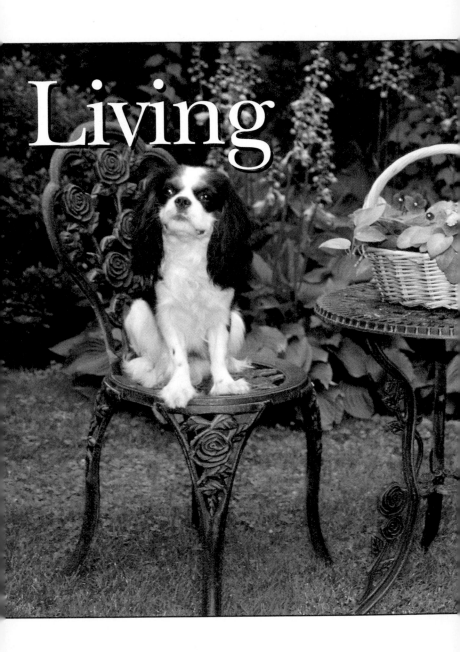

Living

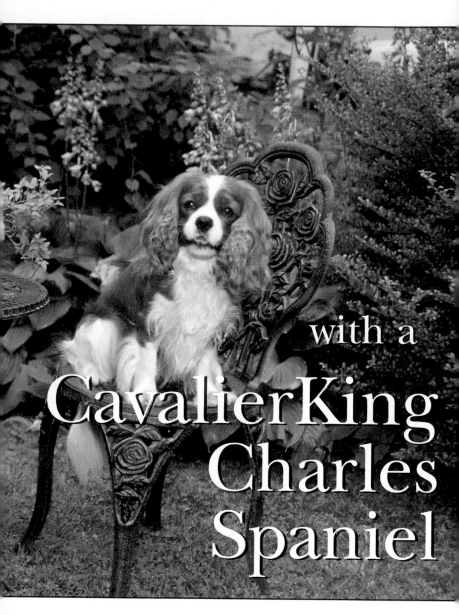

with a

CavalierKing Charles Spaniel

chapter 4

Bringing Your

Cavalier

Home

In the excitement of getting your new Cavalier, don't forget that there is much preparation you must do before those little paws begin to patter around your kitchen. A visit to a pet-supply store with its vast array of merchandise is quite bewildering, unless you have a firm idea of the basic items you will need.

The first essential is a suitable crate, which will provide your puppy with a safe haven and you with an excellent tool for housetraining. Remember that your 4-pound puppy will

36

grow to an adult size of about 18 pounds, and will measure about 13 inches at the shoulder. The crate you buy should be geared to the adult size so that you will not incur the extra expense of purchasing another crate as the puppy grows. There are two types of crates, and both have their advantages. A metal wire crate is a good choice for the kitchen because that is usually where the family spends a lot of time. Your puppy will have company and be able to see what is going on in all directions, while you will be able to notice if she is getting restless and needs to be whisked outside to do her duty.

PUPPY ESSENTIALS

Your new puppy will need:

food bowl

water bowl

collar

leash

ID tag

bed

crate

toys

grooming supplies

If you wish to keep your puppy in the bedroom at night to reassure her and to monitor her need to go out, the "suitcase" type of metal crate is ideal; it folds down quickly and easily to be taken from place to place. For travel in the car, a plastic or fiberglass crate is a safer choice. Its smooth surfaces will provide better protection for the puppy in case of a sudden stop or an accident. There is quite a variation in the quality of plastic crates, and I recommend that you get a really heavy-duty one with a metal mesh door—it may be more expensive but it will not break down with constant use. The flimsier crates often have plastic doors that will go quickly out of alignment with the frame, or plastic catches that will not stand up to wear and tear. When a puppy is teething, a flimsy plastic door is just the thing on which to exercise her sharp new choppers, and in the long run the teeth will win out over the door.

There are all sorts of pads made to fit most crates. The most important feature of a pad for a crate is its ability to stand up to constant washing and drying. Some crate cushions have an inner and outer cover. The inner one cannot be washed and is filled with substances such as cedar to repel fleas. These have a zippered outer cover that can be removed for washing. I recommend the all-in-one, totally washable pad because it is really more hygienic to be able to put the whole thing in the washer and be sure it is clean right through. A puppy will enjoy her own nice cozy cushion in any room of the house. One bed I recommend you avoid is the wicker basket with cushion. The puppy will inevitably chew on the wicker, which will splinter badly. A sharp piece could pierce your puppy's tongue or mouth, or if ingested could get stuck in the stomach or intestine.

Where to Keep Your Puppy?

Having settled the matter of the puppy's crate and pad, the next consideration is what equipment you need to let her out of the crate but still keep her in a confined area of the house. The kitchen is ideal because of its washable floor, and if there is no door between the kitchen and other rooms of the house, a baby gate will be indispensable to prevent the puppy from bouncing all over the house to the detriment of your rugs or broadloom. Even if there is a door to the kitchen, you can leave it open and install a baby gate because the puppy will be able to see you through the gate and be reassured by your presence.

A crate is essential for your new puppy.

A shut door is an invitation to the puppy to scratch to attract your attention. A plastic pressure-fitted gate with diagonal mesh is probably the best kind for this purpose, since a wooden one is just too tempting for a chewing puppy. Beware of a wooden gate with vertical slats—a puppy can get her head stuck between the slats, causing panic or even injury if she is alone at the time. Most baby gates have a spring-release, one-handed operation, which makes them easy to open and close. If the mechanism is awkward or difficult to operate you may find yourself climbing the gate instead with the likelihood of injury to yourself.

An alternative to the baby gate is an enclosed exercise pen that can be set up in the kitchen with the puppy bed at one end and thick newspapers at the other— just in case. Between the bed and the newspapers place a towel lengthwise so that the floor of the exercise pen has good traction for the puppy's feet so that she will not slip on the kitchen floor and strain her young joints and legs. "Ex" pens are made of six or eight wire mesh foldable panels, some with doors and some with-out. A door is preferable, so that the puppy does not have to be lifted in and out, but it does add to the cost of the pen. A pen 24 inches high is about right for the Cavalier and for you. Any higher, and those panels can be hard on the midriff when you bend over them to

A deep, narrow water bowl will help in keeping your Cavalier's ears dry when she's thirsty.

pick up your puppy. The "Ex" pen has one advantage in that the puppy is totally confined and unable to get into any hazards while you are out.

Other Essentials

Other essential purchases are water and food bowls, and there are many to choose from— plastic, porcelain or stainless steel. The porcelain ones are usu-

ally prettily decorated but very breakable, while the colorful plastic ones are eminently chewable. That leaves the stainless steel bowls which, though not pleas-ing to the eye, are not only indestructible but can be put into the dishwasher and made thoroughly sanitary. It is important that a well-filled water dish be wherever your puppy is. There is a special water dish designed for the crate or pen that sits in its own holder and can be adjusted to the puppy's height as she grows.

When selecting a water or food dish, remember that your Cavalier will grow long feathered ears. A deep, rather narrow bowl is preferable to a wide one that allows the ears to be covered in whatever the dish holds. A dish 4 to 5 inches wide and about 2 inches high is ideal.

What's a Snood?

As your puppy loses her fluffy coat and begins to grow those lovely long ears that frame the face, you may want to buy her a snood to wear while she is eating, so that

her ears will remain pristine. The snood is a kind of little elasticized hat that you pull on over her nose and eyes to the top of the head to hold the ears up and out of her food, and these are available also at many pet stores. They have the added charm of making your Cavalier look like a little Victorian lady in a mob cap. The use of a snood must begin very early in the puppy's life so that she gets used to the routine of having it put on before she eats.

Collars and Leads

Now to the equipment needed for the puppy herself. It is very basic indeed, and consists of a collar

Make sure that your Cavalier is on a lead at all times when she is outside.

and two kinds of lead. Pay a little visit to your puppy at the breeder's home about a week before she is due to come home to you. Measure the circumference of her neck with a piece of string, and then you will have no trouble selecting the right size collar. Buy her a flat nylon adjustable collar that has room to expand, with a quick-release plastic buckle. While her coat is relatively short, this type of collar is suitable, but when she begins to grow long hair as an adult a rolled nylon or leather collar is preferable to avoid cutting the coat.

A simple buckle collar is the first step in control, and the second is the lead. A 4-to-6-foot lead about the same width of the collar should be perfect because it is the type of lead used in most puppy training classes. Collar-and-lead sets come in every shade of the rainbow, to say nothing of snazzy embroidered sets. You can have fun deciding which of these will enhance your puppy's looks and personality.

Have an identification tag made for the collar with your name and telephone number on it in case the puppy strays and is lost. The tag can be put on a new collar as your puppy grows. The second lead you purchase should be a retractable one, which will give your puppy some freedom of movement while keeping her under control. These leads have a plastic handgrip and a nylon running line 12 to 26 feet in length. The line will automatically extend and retract as your puppy runs away from you and back again. If there is a sudden emergency, you can stop the line from running free by putting the thumb-operated brake on, and you can reel her in quickly.

Toys!

A small Kong provides an excellent way for your puppy to pass the time. It is a hard rubber toy with an irregular shape and a hole on the underside. With peanut butter spread inside, or stuffed with some other treat, it will have your puppy licking and chewing with enjoyment for hours. Kongs are also great for throwing and retrieving because they bounce unpredictably, giving your puppy the pleasure of the chase. A hard rubber ball is perfect for the game of "fetch" but be sure the ball is large enough so that it can't get stuck in the puppy's throat, and small enough for her to get a good grip on it.

One inexpensive toy I have found that is wonderful for puppy play and encourages retrieving is a child's "splash ball." These are the size of tennis balls, made for children to soak with water and throw at each other. They are polyester filled and covered with nylon material, very light to handle and spongy soft. Because they are so light, when a puppy pounces, the ball will skitter off to entice the puppy to pounce again. When she does pick it up it is so soft she can carry it easily. Ariel, a Blenheim puppy now 7 months old, is addicted

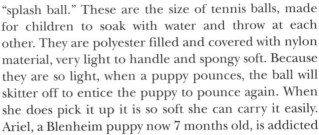

to the splash ball. She will carry it around all day, as a child will carry a favorite doll, and offer it to any visitor to throw for her.

A toy that costs the owner nothing is a pair of old wool socks tied together. A puppy will carry this around, growling and shaking it as though it were alive. Another good type of plaything is a tug toy, which is ideal for play

*Toys should be
fun—but safe.*

between you and your puppy—but don't leave her alone with it. The tug toys are usually made of cotton or nylon, tightly braided, so the puppy cannot ingest any large amount, but it is wise to err on the side of caution and take it away when you have finished the game of tug-of-war.

Toys to Avoid

Toys to avoid are those made of soft plastic, or those that have squeakers in them, unless you are there to supervise the play. Many an owner has suffered grief after a teething puppy chewed off a large piece of plastic or a squeaker and swallowed it, thus blocking the intestine. Soft plastic toys made in the shape of steaks, hot dogs and cute figures are gimmicks made to appeal to the owner, but the purchase of these should be resisted because the puppy's safety is paramount.

Puppy-Proofing the Yard

Now that you have your puppy's needs inside the house taken care of, begin to look around your yard to be sure it is puppy-proof. Whether you have a small yard or a garden, you need to take a walk around the perimeter, looking for small openings or spaces where an adventurous Cavalier puppy could squeeze through. If there is any space between fence and ground you can be sure that the puppy will find it. She will squeeze her nose into the smallest gap and then wiggle her way under the opening like a snake.

Do you have a prized flower or vegetable section of your garden? If so, fence it off with some chicken wire. Freshly turned soil is an invitation to digging for your Cavalier, which will mean a trip to the bathtub for her, and rescue of your upended plants. Cavaliers are not constant diggers, but the smell of well-cultivated soil is irresistible to most dogs. If your puppy does turn out to be a digger and makes holes in your lawn, you can thwart her easily. Fill the hole with her poop and cover it with a thin layer of earth. I guarantee she will not go back to dig in that hole again.

Speaking of poop, one other set of equipment absolutely necessary to the new puppy owner is a poop-scoop set consisting of two long-handled implements. One has a flat blade on one side and it is used to push the poop into the small pan on the end of the other. At least one cleanup of the yard is needed every

HOUSEHOLD DANGERS

Curious puppies and inquisitive dogs get into trouble not because they are bad, but simply because they want to investigate the world around them. It's our job to protect our dogs from harmful substances, like the following:

In the Garage

antifreeze

garden supplies, like snail and slug bait, pesticides, fertilizers and mouse and rat poisons

In the House

cleaners, especially pine oil

perfumes, colognes and aftershaves

medications and vitamins

office and craft supplies

electric cords

chicken and turkey bones

chocolate and onions

some house and garden plants, like ivy, oleander and poinsettia

day, as a puppy will have to eliminate three or four times a day. Don't let the poop accumulate because there is nothing worse than having a puppy trot through her feces on a wet day, then walk her into the house. If this happens fairly often, your house will soon be permeated with doggy odor that you may not notice, but your visitors surely will. An accumulation of feces in a yard will bring flies and the possibility of disease for your family as well as for the dog.

Another excellent reason for poop-scooping often is that your Cavalier will be discouraged from eating her own poop. Coprophagy, or poop eating, is not a common habit among Cavaliers, but the occasional dog will do it, and there is no telling which dogs will develop this habit.

Now that you have puppy-proofed your house and yard, you wait with anticipation for the day when you will bring your darling Cavalier home. It will be a learning experience for her and your family, and there are a number of good ideas to make the transition from the breeder's home to yours a pleasant one.

Early Days with Your Puppy

It is important that someone in the family be able to be at home during the first early weeks when the puppy needs the most attention and instruction. It is an intensive period because from 8 to 16 weeks of age the puppy is a little learning sponge, soaking up all the information and acquiring the habits that will last a lifetime.

As an illustration of how a puppy can learn a lifetime habit at a very young age, there is the story of our dancing Cavalier, Ollie. He came to us at 8 weeks old, a happy and outgoing tricolor boy. I noticed that, even at this early age, Ollie was agile and could keep his balance on two back feet for a few moments at a time. Judicious use of a biscuit as an incentive soon had Ollie turning in circles on two feet, and in short order he was pirouetting from one side of the room to the other. Ollie was always anxious to perform his party trick and it was particularly popular with visiting children. All we had to say was "Ollie, dance!" and off he would go to the delight of all watchers. As he grew old and arthritis took its toll, we had to stop asking him to dance, but occasionally he would try without being asked in the hopes of getting a cookie. Needless to say, our dear Ollie received many cookies to prevent his getting up on his old legs. Fortunately, Ollie was thin by nature and the extra cookies did him no harm.

Spending Time with Your Puppy

Time spent with a young puppy will pay off in good behavior and good citizenship for life. There is nothing sadder than a new puppy being left at home alone while everyone is out of the house during the day. Apart from the fact that she is desperately lonely and pining for company, when someone does come home she will go mad with excitement and be difficult to control. A family at work or school all day has only a couple of hours in the morning and a few at night, and little time to give a puppy the socializing and training she needs. Families with children, in particular, have busy evenings and weekends with group activities of all kinds. Look carefully at your schedule to see if you really have enough time to devote to her. As a breeder, I have a firm policy never to sell a Cavalier to anyone if there is nobody home during the day.

Bringing Your Puppy Home

Presuming that the matter of providing time for the puppy has been dealt with, you are just waiting for the day when you can make your Cavalier a member of the family. When that day arrives, pick up your puppy in the morning so that she has the entire day to get used to her new people and location. A puppy brought home in the evening and put to bed in a strange house all by herself is liable to make a fuss about the abrupt change. She has never been alone in her life; her mother and her littermates have always been there to snuggle up with and make her feel secure.

Puppies in general, and Cavaliers in particular, benefit from a regular schedule during the day, which helps immensely with housetraining. On arriving home with your puppy, carry her from the car to the spot in the backyard where you want her to do her business. It is likely that she will want to relieve herself, and when she

does, praise her immediately. Puppies are natural fol-
lowers because they are pack animals. Encourage her to
follow you into the house and to the kitchen where you
have set up her living area. Playing on the floor at puppy
level is the best way to begin the social interaction that
makes the special link between Cavalier and owners.

Impress upon everyone who is going to play with the
puppy the importance of not getting her overexcited.
Supervise children whenever they play with her to
be sure that neither they nor the puppy has a bad
experience.

Puppy Chewing

Like other dogs, the Cavalier puppy learns about the
world mostly through teeth and nose. She will chew on
anything, and human fingers come in nicely for this
experiment. One instruction I like to give to the new
owner and the family is that of knowing how to deal
with a puppy that wants to bite down on fingers. As
soon as she closes her jaws on you, leave your hand or
finger in her mouth but give a loud high-pitched
scream. The noise will startle her and she will let go.
The very instant she lets go, praise her. Next, offer your
finger or hand to her to see if she will try again. If she
does, go through the same routine. The key is not to
pull your hand away, and this is sometimes difficult to
teach to children, but it is well worth persisting with
this method of bite-proofing the puppy. The upshot of
this training causes the dog to realize that the human
is very tender and must not be chewed on. Though this
is only the puppy's first lesson, training in all aspects of
her life will be necessary. Chapter 8 will give you a
good grounding on how to train your Cavalier to be
both a good pet and a good canine citizen.

Naptime

When the puppy seems tired from her introduction to
house, new family and a playtime, put her into her
crate for a nap. Never let anyone wake her up to play
with her. She needs to sleep her tiredness away as

human babies do, and if woken frequently at the whim of children, will become nervous and cranky. When she wakes up, she will want to go to the toilet and will probably cry to get out of the crate because she will want to keep her bed clean.

From the time my puppies are on their feet at the age of 3 weeks they will creep out of their bed and totter over to the newspaper at the end of the exercise pen to do their duty. When she cries to get out, carry her again to the chosen spot in the yard. Cavalier puppies are toy size and bladders and intestines are correspondingly small. While she is awake and playing she will have to relieve herself every twenty minutes or so. Getting her out frequently is the key.

Some puppies will just like to stop and smell the flowers.

A sleeping puppy can go through the night for six hours or so without having to be taken out. The pattern of crate time and play, interspersed with three meals a day at this age, is a routine that your puppy will adapt to quickly, and she will become so attuned to it that she will soon be able to tell you that you are late with her dinner by dancing around and asking for it.

When you put your new puppy to bed on her first night in your home, you will set a pattern for the rest of her life. It is not fair to exile her to a crate in the laundry room or basement where she is totally alone, feels abandoned and cries her little heart out. The best routine is to take her crate into your own bedroom so that you can reassure her that she is not alone, and to be aware if she needs to go out in the night.

On the other hand, you may have decided that this puppy is to have the privilege of sleeping on the bottom of your own bed with the idea that if it was good enough for King Charles II it's good enough for you. In our house the dogs take turns on our bed, two at a

47

time. The rule is that both must sleep on the same side and must not creep up above our elbows. In fact, Cavaliers do love to work their way up the bed to your face, and many would love to sleep curled around your head if you would allow it, rather like a little Cavalier bonnet. Whatever your decision, the idea is to have the puppy somewhere near you at night because she needs to know you are there and ready to care for her

VISITING THE VETERINARIAN

After a few days of settling in to her new routine you should take your Cavalier puppy to your vet. The conscientious breeder has done everything right for this puppy, such as deworming and first vaccination, but it is a good idea to have your own veterinarian check her out. There is also the advantage of introducing your puppy to the veterinarian in a pleasurable way when there is no problem to address, so that the puppy will be able to associate a trip to the vet with a sociable visit. No doubt she will greet the vet as she does all other humans, and have her wrapped around her royal paw in no time.

If the visit to your veterinarian does indeed turn up any kind of problem, the breeder should be the first person to know. In such a case it is a good idea to ask the breeder to talk directly to your veterinarian for the information. While you are investigating veterinarians, always ask about their after hours emergency services. Some veterinarians band together and take turns for out of office hours calls, and these are usually a group who live in a common area. The advantage here is that these veterinarians usually know each other personally, and as well as providing a written report will talk to each other about any emergency problem your Cavalier has had. There are practices in large urban centers that specialize in emergency care after hours. The veterinarians who tend to work for these organizations are usually new graduates without much experience who are willing to work night hours. For this reason I prefer to locate a group of local veterinarians as described above. Emergency service specialist clinics are usually expensive, but when there is a health emergency for your Cavalier the cost of treatment is usually the last thing you will be considering.

The Benefit of Training

After your puppy's second vaccination, at about the age of 12 weeks, her immunity will be boosted to the point where she can go out to puppy training classes. Your Cavalier will probably be the smallest dog in the class, and this is a good reason to enroll her. Most owners of large, boisterous breeds must take their puppies to these classes to get them under control. The Cavalier, on the other hand, should go because she needs to get used to seeing these other dogs who, to her eyes, may look like monsters about to make a meal of a little royal toy spaniel. She may spend the first week ready to creep under the nearest chair, but after a few sessions with lots of encouragement she will realize that the other dogs are just puppies like her, and before long she will be out there playing with the largest of them without feeling threatened.

All puppy training classes work on basic training using an incentive and reward method, and this is the only kind of training suitable for the Cavalier. She is so very sensitive to the moods of her human that a cross word is all that is needed in the way of correction.

chapter 5

Feeding
Your
Cavalier

Apart from a good set of genes and a strong constitution, what determines the state of health and longevity of your Cavalier is nutrition. Over the years, I have discovered that more problems develop from oversupplementation rather than lack of nutrition. We are so concerned about getting everything right, to give a puppy all he can eat, to add oil supplements to give a shiny coat or take the word of a friend that this or that will give your dog optimum health. As with all things in life, there is a balance to be found in all this advice and information about feeding your dog.

Complete Dry Food Versus Natural Feeding

Large commercial dog food companies spend millions of dollars and do the experimentation necessary to be sure that their food is nutritious and will be suitable for the average dog. My only quarrel with them is that they advertise that their foods give complete nutrition. From a chemical point of view this may well be the case, but if you were to offer the average Cavalier a bowl of dry dog food and a bowl of minced meat, what do you think he would choose? The taste and enjoyment of meat will win out every time.

Meat by itself, of course, is not sufficient. In the wild, dogs would eat the partly digested contents of an animal's stomach, and that, along with the rest of the carcass, would provide the right diet. Our dogs are totally dependent upon what we provide for them, so how do we give them as close to a natural diet as possible? As with all else, compromise is the key.

In addition to a good-quality dry kibble food, I always add a couple of tablespoons of ground or chunk meat and 1 teaspoon per dog of raw pureed vegetables, all mixed together with a little water to moisten. The vegetable mixture I use is mostly broccoli and carrots. Dogs cannot digest the cellulose contained in a whole carrot, for instance, but if you puree that carrot the dog's digestive system can assimilate a good part of it.

TYPES OF FOODS/TREATS

There are three types of commercially available dog food—dry, canned and semisoft—and a huge assortment of treats (lucky dogs) to feed your dog. Which should you choose?

Dry and canned foods contain similar ingredients. The primary difference between them is their moisture content. The moisture is not just water; it's blood and broth, too, the very things that dogs adore. So while canned food is more palatable, dry food is more economical, convenient and effective in controlling tartar buildup. Most owners feed a 25% canned/75% dry diet to give their dogs the benefit of both. Just be sure your dog is getting the nutrition he needs (you and your veterinarian can determine this).

Semi-moist foods have the flavor dogs love and the convenience owners want. However, they tend to contain excessive amounts of artificial colors and preservatives.

Dog treats come in every size, shape and flavor imaginable, from organic cookies shaped like postmen to beefy chew sticks. Dogs seem to love them all, so enjoy the variety. Just be sure not to overindulge your dog. Factor treats into his regular meal sizes.

There is some controversy as to whether the meat given to your dog should be raw or cooked. I prefer to give raw meat because it is his natural food and much more digestible for the dog. However, in hot climates, and for reasons of safety, many people prefer to cook the meat before feeding it. In thirty years of feeding dogs, I have never had a problem with giving them raw meat, but I am very careful that it is fresh, and any uneaten portion is thrown out right away. If you wish to feed raw ground or stewing beef, it is easy to buy a pound at a time, then make it into small portions which can be frozen and pulled out of the freezer on the day of use. If you are a pet owner and have just one Cavalier, the cost of fresh beef is a small outlay to be sure your dog is getting good-quality meat.

Ingredients Good Enough to Eat

When selecting a dry food for your Cavalier, read the label and see what the ingredients are. First of all, in a puppy or active adult diet, meat should be the first ingredient because it provides the essential protein. Protein levels vary from 15 percent for older dogs to 26 or 28 percent for puppies. On the whole, a protein count in dry food of 21 to 23 percent is suitable for the adult Cavalier.

A small amount of table scraps can be added to a meal if the scraps consist of meat or cooked vegetables other than potato, but leftover bones must never be given. Bones of any kind are attractive to any dog, but cooked bones of any kind are deadly—they will splinter if chewed and can easily pierce the stomach or intestines. You should not only put them into the garbage, but stuff them well down in the bin so that a brief raid by Charlie won't retrieve them. Raw sliced beef shank marrow bones are the only safe ones for your Cavalier.

How Much Food Is Enough?

How much food is right for the Cavalier? A young puppy needs three meals a day, and he should be allowed to eat all he can in about ten to fifteen minutes. After that, pick up the dish and keep any remaining food in the refrigerator until the next meal. The exception to this rule is a puppy that adores his food and soon becomes very fat. He should not be given the opportunity to eat as much as he likes but should be rationed until he slims down a little and then should be given enough to maintain a slow and steady weight gain. You will notice, at about the age of 4 months, the puppy will begin to pick away at one of those three meals, instead of eating with enthusiasm. When this happens, you know it is time to put him on two meals a day, one in the morning and one in the evening. The same general rule applies about letting him eat all he can in a limited time. Once he is past 6 months of age, you can safely put him on an adult meal of about one cup of food a day in the late afternoon or early evening, with just a snack of a cookie or two in the morning.

Watching Your Dog's Weight

Now you must use the "rule of eye and hand," which means that you should be able to see your Cavalier's waist just behind the ribs, and you should be able to feel the ribs, but not see them. A good general rule for an adult Cavalier is to feed one cup of food a day. If your Cavalier begins to look like a sausage with no shape to his body, cut down on the food right away. Females in particular are very good

---

HOW TO READ THE DOG FOOD LABEL

With so many choices on the market, how can you be sure you are feeding the right food to your dog? The information is all there on the label—if you know what you're looking for.

Look for the nutritional claim right up top. Is the food "100 percent nutritionally complete?" If so, it's for nearly all life stages; "growth and maintenance," on the other hand, is for early development. Puppy foods and foods for senior dogs are specially marked so you can choose the proper food for your dog's stage.

Ingredients are listed in descending order by weight. The first three or four ingredients will tell you the bulk of what the food contains. Look for the highest-quality ingredients, like meats and grains, to be among them.

The Guaranteed Analysis tells you what levels of protein, fat, fiber and moisture are in the food, in that order. While these numbers are meaningful, they won't tell you much about the quality of the food. Nutritional value is in the dry matter, not the moisture content.

In many ways, seeing is believing. If your dog has bright eyes, a shiny coat, a good appetite and a good energy level, chances are his diet's fine. Your dog's breeder and your veterinarian are good sources of advice if you're still not sure which food is appropriate.

eaters and efficient users of their food and are prone to put on weight easily. I have several Cavalier girls who thrive and look just right on two-thirds of a cup of food a day. They gobble their ration and then just look at me with those huge, soulful brown eyes as if to say "Is that all there is?" I have to steel myself not to give in—if it is hard for me as a breeder to keep them to their diet, then it is going to be even harder for you as a pet owner when those eyes go through the begging routine. You may find that giving two tiny meals a day, totaling half the usual quantity, is easier on both you and the dog.

A fat Cavalier is one whose life will be short and unhealthy because of the genetic tendency in the breed to heart disease (see Chapter 6, "Keeping Your Cavalier Healthy"). It is unusual for a Cavalier to be a picky eater, but it does happen occasionally, and it is usually a male who has this problem. I hear from owners that they have gone through many brands of food to find one that their Cavalier will eat. On the introduction of a new food the dog will eat for a day or so, then go back to the old habit of being picky. The frustrated owners then try adding a good quantity of chicken or beef to tempt the appetite. Well, that smart dog picks out the meat and leaves the rest.

HOW MANY MEALS A DAY?

Individual dogs vary in how much they should eat to maintain a desired body weight—not too fat, but not too thin. Puppies need several meals a day, while older dogs may only need one. Determine how much food keeps your adult dog looking and feeling his best. Then decide how many meals you want to feed with that amount. Like us, most dogs love to eat, and offering two meals a day is more enjoyable for them. If you're worried about overfeeding, make sure you measure correctly and abstain from adding tidbits to the meals.

Whether you feed one or two meals, only leave your dog's food out for the amount of time it takes him to eat it—ten minutes, for example. Free-feeding (when food's available any time) and leisurely meals encourage picky eating. Don't worry if your dog doesn't finish all his dinner in the allotted time. He'll learn he should.

No Finicky Eaters

My advice is to stick to one good brand of food, mixed with a small amount of meat and vegetable as described before, put the dish down and pick it up after fifteen minutes whether it is still full or not. The dog may go for nearly twenty-four hours without eating more than a bite or two, but don't give in. Throw out what has not been eaten and give him another meal at the proper time. He may get very thin indeed, but he will not starve himself, and you must try not to worry. Above all, don't tempt him with any special goodies and don't give him any treats whatsoever because then he will expect these all the time and will turn his nose up at the regular fare.

Keep the Oldies Slim

Diet for the older Cavalier requires that the protein count be reduced to about 15 percent, and that the food contain little or no salt. Most Cavaliers past their middle years will be spayed or neutered, their lives will be less active, and these are other good reasons to take special care not to overfeed. When I was a novice breeder and more experienced, people told me that spayed or neutered dogs put on weight more readily than others, and I thought that was just an old wives'

Your Cavalier will be a welcome guest at any formal function. (photo by Norma Moffat)

tale. Now I know that what they said is true. It seems that when the hormones are not working, the metabolic processes change, and any weight gained is hard to lose, particularly if the dog is past middle age.

To Bone or Not to Bone

You will find that though your Cavalier enjoys his food, he will still have the need to chew. Modern food does not allow for the kind of chewing that is beneficial to teeth and gums. The matter of giving bones to Cavaliers is a contentious issue, some breeders swear by bones and some breeders swear at them and tell their puppy owners never to allow the dog to have any bone at all. In my opinion, after thirty years in dogs and nearly twenty in Cavaliers, the only type of bone I will allow my Cavaliers to have is a piece of raw beef shank marrow bone. There is no danger of splintering with this bone, and the dogs have the added satisfaction of being able to lick the nutritious marrow out of the middle. I have the butcher cut the shank into pieces 1 to $1^1/_2$ inches long. I keep them in the freezer and take them out on the day I wish to feed them. My dogs have them as a treat once a week, and it keeps them happy for at least an hour's good gnawing. The great advantage is that while it satisfies their desire to chew it cleans the teeth and tones up the gums. From a sanitary point of view, beef marrow bones must always be taken away and thrown out once the dog has had the marrow out of the middle and a good chew. No other bones of any description should be given to a Cavalier because of the danger of splintering and internal injury.

Cavaliers absolutely adore the pig's ear chewy treats that are available at every pet supply store, and I must confess to buying these occasionally. The problem is that they are very greasy and will make a mess of Cavalier ears unless you have trained your dog to tolerate a snood. Hard dog cookies will provide some jaw exercise, but since the Cavalier is prone to put on weight, these must be strictly limited. Dog cookie manufacturers add extra flavorings and sugar to make their product toothsome, but the calories added to the daily total in one cookie can be really detrimental to an already pudgy Cavalier.

TO SUPPLEMENT OR NOT TO SUPPLEMENT?

If you're feeding your dog a diet that's correct for his developmental stage and he's alert, healthy looking and neither over- nor underweight, you don't need to add supplements. These include table scraps as well as vitamins and minerals. In fact, unless you are a nutrition expert, using food supplements can actually hurt a growing puppy. For example, mixing too much calcium into your dog's food can lead to musculoskeletal disorders. Educating yourself about the quantity of vitamins and minerals your dog needs to be healthy will help you determine what needs to be supplemented. If you have any concerns about the nutritional quality of the food you're feeding, discuss them with your veterinarian.

Dangerous Treats

On the subject of dog treats, there are so many kinds marketed to appeal to the owner rather than the dog, including some that are advertised as "chocolate drops." This treat is not chocolate, but a carob substitute that can be well tolerated by dogs. In fact, real chocolate must never be used as a treat because it contains the chemical theobromine, which can be toxic. One Christmas my daughter's Cavalier, Trixie, inclined to be fat and known to be a clever food thief, discovered a 1-pound box of very expensive chocolates and scoffed the lot. The family was out at the time, and they came home to find poor Trixie feeling quite sick and sorry for herself, but alive. The reason she survived was that she had promptly vomited her stolen meal all over the living room carpet. In spite of cleaning, that carpet retained the mark of Trixie's bout with chocolate for the rest of its days. I have had several terribly sad telephone calls from my puppy owners who have lost dogs through chocolate poisoning, and I cannot urge you too strongly to be careful and in particular to explain to children that they should never treat their Cavalier with a piece of their chocolate bar.

Your Cavalier will love treats, but make sure that he doesn't put on too much extra weight.

Another food that it is well not to give is cheese such as cheddar or mozzarella. A breeder friend of mine was slicing cheese, and as his three dogs began to beg for a piece, he cut off a chunk for each and they went off happily wagging to eat it. He found one of them dead a few minutes later because it had tried to bolt the piece whole. The cheese had partly melted, covered the breathing passages and the dog suffocated.

The Essential Nature of Water

We cannot leave the subject of feeding your Cavalier without mentioning the importance of readily available water to help your dog's digestive processes. I cannot emphasize enough the essential nature of water for the dog. Your dog can survive well for days without food, but not without water. Wherever your Cavalier is, whether in your kitchen, in your car or visiting friends, always have water sitting in a bowl nearby so that he can slake his thirst. When you are visiting, always take water from home for your pet. As with humans, a change of water can sometimes cause stomach upsets or diarrhea, and this can be avoided by always carrying a bottle of water with you. If you are traveling in the car there is an ingenious plastic water dish commonly known as a "water hole." It has a small opening in the top just big enough for your Cavalier's muzzle to go in easily, and a wide rim with a curve down towards the center. The "water hole" type of dish can be carried uncovered in the car, and it won't spill over when the car is in motion.

Milk

On the subject of liquids, I am often asked if milk is beneficial for dogs. Adult Cavaliers do not need milk in any form, excepting the pregnant female who can benefit from the extra calcium. Cow's milk should not be given because the type of lactose it contains is not digestible and will probably cause diarrhea. Goat's milk, however, is readily digestible by both young and old, and I have never seen a case of stomach upset when using it. Goat's milk in the quart size is becoming commonly available in supermarkets, and it is carried in many health food stores. I mix goat milk with soaked puppy food when weaning young puppies, and they seem to thrive on it.

chapter 6

Grooming
Your
Cavalier

The Cavalier is a natural breed requiring minimal—but regular—grooming to keep it looking its best. The coat of the unneutered animal is medium in length, with long feathering on the ears, chest, legs, tail and feet. The coat is straight and silky, easy to care for and is often referred to as "wash and wear" by breeders. The AKC Breed Standard does not allow any trimming of show specimens, but this may be necessary when

dealing with a neutered pet, as neutering causes excess coat growth, and a change in the feel of the coat, which is finer and thicker, rather like cotton than silk.

Equipment

Before we begin a discussion of the actual process of grooming, some information is necessary about the tools you will need to do the grooming easily and efficiently.

Grooming Table   While a table of this kind is not essential, it does make the job of grooming so much

easier. These tables are available at any pet-supply store, are foldable and can be put away in a cupboard when not in use. The height of the table is just right so that you will be able to avoid bending your back, and it is covered with rubber matting providing a washable surface, yet giving the dog secure footing. It is a

It is important to have a range of grooming equipment.

good idea to buy a grooming arm that has a c-clamp to fix it to the table. From the grooming arm hangs an adjustable dog collar, which will allow you to keep both hands free for grooming.

Combs   The best type of comb for a Cavalier is a small one, about 5 inches in length, one half having wide spaced teeth and the other half more closely placed teeth. It may be advertised in pet-supply catalogs as a cat comb. The wide tooth half is good for general combing, and the narrower end can be used for combing out the fine hair behind the ears, and to pull out fleas should you ever have a summer infestation. Since I try to raise my Cavaliers in a natural way, I never use insecticidal chemicals directly on my dogs, but instead use a premise spray for carpets, crates and baseboards. Then I comb every dog every day until the pesky critters are gone. When you go to the store to buy a comb, run your fingers over the ends of the teeth. The teeth should not feel sharp to the touch, but should be rounded so that they do not tear the coat.

Brushes   There are three brushes that have different functions, and all are necessary in the grooming of your Cavalier. The first is an oval-headed "pin" brush, about 7 inches long from end to end, which has a rubber cushion inset with metal pins. If you only buy one brush for your Cavalier, the pin brush is the one to have because it is used most often in general grooming. Next comes the slicker brush which has a square flat head covered with very fine pins, like a carding comb. Cavalier ears and feathering tangle easily, and use of the slicker will encourage all those tangled hairs to lie in the same direction, and then they can be combed out. Last comes the finishing touch, a bristle brush. The other brushes prepare the coat so that it lays flat and tangle free, but the bristle brush is the one that will provide that silky sheen so typical of the Cavalier coat.

Nail Clippers There are two types of clippers available on the market, one a guillotine type with one blade, while the other has two cutting edges. I find the clipper with two cutting edges much easier to use. The guillotine type requires that the dog's nail be inserted into a hole cut in the end of the clipper, then the blade is depressed to cut the nail. Unless you have a very steady hand it is easy to put too much of the nail through the hole and cut into the quick. It is very difficult to use this clipper with a dog that objects to the process. The two-blade clipper works like scissors and has a guard so that you cannot cut the nail past the quick.

Scissors The Cavalier is a natural breed that should be left untrimmed, but it is allowable to cut off excess hair on the underneath of the foot. Long hair left to accumulate between the pads will mat and form a slippery cushion, giving the dog poor traction. It will also retain water, which is unhealthy for the pads since they should dry off quickly after getting wet to avoid bacterial infections between the toes. Small scissors with rounded ends are the best solution for trimming

---

GROOMING TOOLS

pin brush
slicker brush
flea comb
towel
mat rake
grooming glove
scissors
nail clippers
tooth-cleaning equipment
shampoo
conditioner
clippers

---

under the feet. If you cannot find them in a pet-supply store you may very well come across them in your supermarket's baby supply section where they're sold as baby nail scissors.

Grooming Spray Since you should never groom a Cavalier coat when it is dry, a grooming spray is essential. There are many to choose from in pet-supply stores, but the one I prefer is a skin conditioner as well as a grooming spray. It contains tea tree oil (melaleuca alternifolia), which is healing for the skin and has the added benefit of discouraging fleas and mites, which hate the eucalyptus odor. It is well to experiment with several types of grooming spray to determine which one is best for your dog. There are sprays specially made for sensitive skin which contain aloe vera or other soothing ingredients.

Shampoos and Conditioners It is important that you do not use human shampoos and conditioners on your Cavalier. The ph level of the dog's skin is different from yours, and what is suitable for you may be highly irritating for her. Whatever shampoo you select, be sure that it is gentle and not drying to the coat. My favorite has a base of coconut oil, which gives a lovely sheen and a pleasant lingering scent. The main purpose of conditioners is to be anti-static, tame the fly-away coat and help to prevent tangles from forming. I

Regular brushing of your Cavalier's teeth will keep them healthy. Be sure to use toothpaste specifically made for dogs.

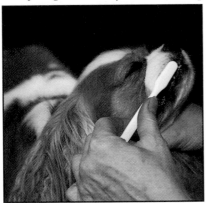

have often simply used the grooming spray liberally after the bath in lieu of conditioner since it does basically the same job.

Toothpaste and Toothbrush Cleaning the teeth is an essential part of the grooming process for a Cavalier. The muzzle is relatively short, yet contains the same number of teeth as that of a German Shepherd or any other large breed, and the teeth are packed closely together. Doggy toothpaste and toothbrush come in a kit, which can be purchased at the pet-supply store. Toothpaste comes in several different flavors that appeal to dogs, such as brewer's yeast, liver and beef. The toothbrush supplied has a big brush at one end and a small one at the other to accommodate any size of mouth. The pet supply store will also carry a rubber finger stall for the same purpose for those dogs who object to a brush in the mouth. The finger stall has little rubber bumps on it which will providing a massaging action for the teeth and gums.

Grooming the Puppy

Though your Cavalier puppy will need very little grooming, if any, go through the process regularly, daily if possible. She will become accustomed to the routine and then when she is grown you will have no trouble at grooming or bath time. If you have no objection to using the kitchen as a location, the kitchen sink and counter are an ideal height for grooming your puppy. Otherwise the laundry tub and counter will do, but the laundry tub usually requires that you bend over for some time while washing and rinsing, and it can be hard on your back. Use a rubber mat on the counter so that the puppy does not feel nervous about standing on a slippery surface. The type of rubber mat you can buy to put in a bathtub is perfect for this purpose. The puppy may not be happy being so far off the ground, but you can reassure her by a gentle but firm grip and soothing words.

You want to make the grooming process a pleasant experience for the puppy. Begin by spritzing her body lightly with the grooming spray. Start combing at her head, then gently down the ears and progressing down the body. Repeat this process with the bristle brush. Lift the ear flaps to make sure that the insides of the ears are pink and glistening and that there is no sign of debris or redness. Lift each of her feet in turn, just so that she gets used to having them handled.

Now go back to the head and see if there is any stain or debris at the inner corners of the eyes. Cavalier eyes are so large and round that the tear ducts sometimes cannot take all the flow of tears that is necessary to keep the eye clear, and they overflow. If there is staining, wipe with a cotton ball dampened with saline solution, but if there is dried debris you may need to use the fine-tooth comb to get it out, then use the damp cotton ball.

Holding her mouth shut, insert your finger gently inside the cheek and rub it along her gums and teeth on both sides. When she gets used to this, you can put a little dog toothpaste on your finger, and then eventually you will be able to insert a brush or finger stall to clean her teeth.

Cutting toenails can be stressful for a puppy, but it must be done on a regular basis, about once every two or three weeks. If you do not keep the toenails short and they grow long and curl over, the whole balance of the leg will be thrown off.

Now that grooming is over, the time comes to decide whether the puppy needs a bath. I am not a believer in bathing when it is not absolutely necessary. If the puppy looks dirty or smells dirty then go ahead; otherwise just grooming is sufficient to clean the coat and spread the natural oils from the skin. Too much bathing will dry the coat, and is an unnecessary stress on a puppy.

Grooming the Adult

Grooming three times a week is ideal under normal circumstances, but if you live in the country where there is long grass and burrs you may need to do it more often.

Begin at the head and clean out the area at the inner corners of the eyes, which often have debris from "Cavalier tears." The tears can accumulate, dry out to a dark color and crusty texture and be quite smelly. I keep cotton balls dampened with hydrogen peroxide for cleaning around the eyes. Be very careful not to get this anywhere near the eyes themselves but only in the small area that is stained. Tear staining cannot be seen on rubies and black and tans, but on particolors who do not have much chestnut or black around the eye, tear stains will show and spoil the look of the face. A routine of using hydrogen peroxide on a regular basis whenever you are grooming may not eliminate the staining, but will keep it under control.

Lift the ears and swab them with a makeup pad moistened with rubbing alcohol. Never use a long cotton swab for this purpose because of the danger of damaging the inner ear if the dog jerks her head.

Hold the mouth shut gently with one hand, and with the other insert a small toothbrush inside the cheek and brush upper and lower back teeth with dog toothpaste. Now pull up the lip on one side and brush the upper side and front teeth and repeat the process on the other side.

Be sure to groom your Cavalier at lease three times a week for maximum coat and skin health.

Next, spray the outside of the ears liberally with grooming solution (cupping your hand around the eye to protect it from the spray) and continue down the body, over the legs and tail, working the solution into the coat with your hands. Comb and pin brush are next, working from the ears backwards, combing first and brushing second. When using the pin brush it is best to do a small section at a time, first brushing against the lie of the hair down to the skin, then with the natural lie of the hair to smooth it down. There may be tangles in the ear, leg or tail feathers that will not come out, and this is where the slicker comes into play. Hold just above the tangle with one hand and work away at it

Living with
a Cavalier
King Charles
Spaniel

with the slicker. It is also effective to tease out the tangle with your fingers and then use the slicker brush.

Check the toenails to see if they need cutting. They should be cut once every two or three weeks. Don't put it off! Pet owners dislike cutting nails because they are afraid that they will cut the quick and hurt the dog. It is essential, however, to keep those toenails short. One reason is that they will not cause so much damage to floors and rugs, but the other more important reason is that they can grow so long that they curl over, cause the dog discomfort, and the whole balance of the leg can be thrown off, causing strain.

How often should you bathe your Cavalier? It depends to a large extent upon where you live. In the country there is clean air and the dirt therefore is "clean dirt" which falls out of the coat easily. Regular grooming as specified should be enough to keep the skin and coat in good condition. The occasional bath may be necessary if the dog has been out, on a muddy day for instance, and is just too dirty to bring into the house. City living requires a regular regimen of bathing because of the pollution of the environment. City dirt is usually oily and particolors in particular get a gray tinge to the white of the coat, which is the sign that a bath is due. Do as much bathing as is absolutely necessary, but no more than that. Too much bathing will strip the coat of its own natural oils and will cause skin irritation.

Be cautious when you clip your Cavalier's toenails—or have your veterinarian do it for you.

How to Bathe the Cavalier

Plan bath time for your Cavalier just after a grooming session. If you bathe before grooming it can be a disaster since any tangles or knots will be made much worse and it will be necessary to cut them out of the coat. The eyes and ears will need to be protected during the bath. A trace of petroleum jelly around the eyes will keep soap and water from this sensitive area and cotton balls

66

lightly coated with baby oil can be placed in the ears to prevent water from getting in and causing discomfort.

Though your Cavalier will happily plunge into a pool or lake, standing in the sink or tub and having a bath is a whole different kettle of dog. She may be nervous about being well up off the floor for a length of time,

or she may be upset at being sprayed from head to toe. You may like the fragrance of the shampoo you are using but she may find it strange or unpleasant. Talk to her reassuringly from the time you put her in the tub until she is lifted out, telling her what you are going to do next. She won't know what you are saying, but your tone of voice and your gentle movements, using as little restraint as possible, will make her feel less tense. The whole idea is to make the bathing process as pleasant as possible so that your Cavalier will be happy when the shampoo bottle comes out.

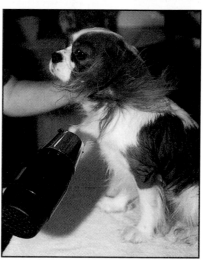

Put a small amount of the shampoo you have chosen into a plastic jug and fill the jug with lukewarm water to dilute it. Using water only, of the same barely warm temperature, wet the dog thoroughly from front to back. Wet hair will absorb the shampoo more readily. Don't use any shampoo from the ears forward, but use a cloth with only water on it to wipe the face, paying particular attention to the upper and lower lips, which sometimes can accumulate debris. Now take the diluted shampoo and beginning at the ears, work your way back along the dog's body, not forgetting to lather under the body and the legs and feet. Rinse off the shampoo until the hair feels squeaky. At this point you can squeeze the

Bathe your Cavalier only when absolutely necessary and make sure to dry her thoroughly afterward.

67

excess water from the coat and apply a diluted cream rinse, about a tablespoon to 2 quarts of rinse. It is safe to leave this in the coat. I prefer to towel dry my dogs and then use a grooming spray instead of a cream rinse, but each method works well.

Drying the coat can be as simple or as elaborate as you wish to make it. After towel drying, run a comb through the damp coat and feathering to reveal any knots that have gone undetected. If you do not require a glamorous show finish and if the weather is warm and sunny, allow her to finish drying by running in the yard. On release from the bathtub into the yard your Cavalier will shake and race around madly, rolling in the grass, and generally telling you how delighted she is to be free of such an unnatural procedure as a bath.

If you wish to have a more professional finish on your dog's coat, or if it is just too cold to let your dog outside to air dry, then a handheld hair dryer is the best tool to use. In any case, don't leave a damp dog to dry by herself in the house. She will take a long time to dry properly in these circumstances and may get a chill. The ears in particular, because the hair is fine and thick, can take almost a whole day to dry and thus be liable to bacterial infections such as canker, which thrive in a warm, damp atmosphere.

When using a dryer, put it on high volume but low heat. Cavaliers are very sensitive to temperature, and a hot air dryer would be painful for the skin. Begin at the ears and use the pin brush to smooth the hair as you dry. When the dog is totally dry, use the bristle brush from head to toe to give a silky finish to the coat. Have some special treat ready as a reward, and give it to the dog as soon as you have finished brushing and while she is still on the table. Now is the time to get out your camera to take a picture of your beautiful Cavalier. One run around the yard and one scratch of the ear will soon return your dog to slightly shaggy, less than perfect looks, but you will have the satisfaction of knowing that she is really clean from head to toe and that the thorough brushing given her skin and coat will be of great benefit to her general health.

chapter 7

Keeping Your **Cavalier** Healthy

From the moment you come home with your new puppy you have the responsibility to be sure that everything is done to keep him in first-class condition. If you have been able to find a veterinarian with other Cavaliers in the practice it will be an advantage because there are specific concerns for the health of the Cavalier that do not occur in other breeds. As mentioned earlier, your first visit should be simply to accustom your puppy to a veterinary visit when no treatment is necessary. At the same time you can inquire about the schedule of fees

for services so that you won't have any unpleasant surprises when you come to pay the bill. While the veterinarian is a busy professional person, he or she should be willing to take time to answer any questions you have and explain about any course of treatment being considered.

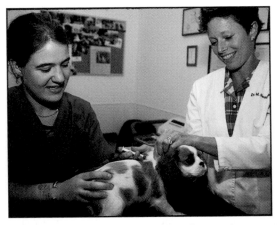

It is very important that you follow up on your puppy's routine vaccinations.

Keep a calendar with the date of your puppy's first vaccination given by the breeder and make an appointment with your veterinarian for twenty-one days from that date for a second booster. Show your veterinarian the first vaccination certificate so that he or she will know what has been given to the puppy previously. At the end of your visit your veterinarian will suggest a schedule of further vaccinations. They should give you a chart with a record of treatment that you will bring back on successive visits to have updated.

Vaccinations

It is important that you keep up a yearly schedule of vaccinations for your Cavalier. Some veterinarians will send you a reminder card so that you can call to make an appointment, but if not then you must make a note on your yearly calendar of the date the dog should receive the yearly booster. Veterinarians use multiple vaccines that will combat a number of the following infectious diseases that in years gone by were fatal to many dogs. In order to emphasize how essential the regular booster vaccine is, here is a list of the diseases vaccinated against, and their symptoms.

Distemper is a highly contagious disease that is viral in origin. Symptoms of distemper include vomiting, diarrhea (and subsequent dehydration) and complete loss of appetite. It is unusual to hear about cases of distemper today since the vaccine is almost 100 percent effective.

Parvovirus is still a danger to dogs today, and outbreaks can occur particularly in the summer months. Even if a dog has been vaccinated it is possible to get the disease but in a less virulent form. The major symptom of Parvo is hemorrhagic diarrhea that smells foul and becomes bloody. Dehydration is rapid, and fluids must be given intravenously. Young puppies that contract Parvo nearly always die within a short period of time because their bodies dehydrate so quickly. Where large numbers of dogs are gathered together in the summer, such as at dog shows where there are feces carried on the feet, Parvo will often be spread.

Coronavirus is a similar virus to Parvo, but less of a threat to adults who can withstand it. It can still be fatal for puppies, however, because the main symptom is severe, continuous diarrhea, in which dehydration is the killer.

Hepatitis primarily attacks the liver, but the kidneys may also be affected by a severe case. It is spread through infected bodily fluids from one dog to another. Dogs affected will be feverish, have painful distended abdomens and yellow jaundice. Intravenous fluids and drugs can be given, but the disease is often fatal.

> ## YOUR PUPPY'S VACCINES
>
> Vaccines are given to prevent your dog from getting infectious diseases like canine distemper or rabies. Vaccines are the ultimate preventive medicine: They're given before your dog ever gets the disease so as to protect him from the disease. That's why it is necessary for your dog to be vaccinated routinely. Puppy vaccines start at 8 weeks of age for the five-in-one DHLPP vaccine and are given every three to four weeks until the puppy is 16 months old. Your veterinarian will put your puppy on a proper schedule and will remind you when to bring in your dog for shots.

Leptospirosis is bacterial in origin. A city-living Cavalier may not need it to be included in the multiple vaccine, but it is necessary for those who live in country areas. The mode of infection is through dogs nosing the dried or fresh urine of rats, foxes, coyotes or other wild animals. Symptoms are fever, loss of appetite and diarrhea. Since it is a bacterial infection, antibiotics are effective against it if given at an early stage.

Parainfluenza, commonly called Kennel Cough, may be bacterial or viral in origin. It is carried by a dog's sneeze or cough, and any dog in his vicinity will be at risk. The veterinarian will usually prescribe antibiotics even though they are ineffective if the cough is viral in origin. Antibiotics, however, will prevent complications of the disease, such as congestion of the lungs. Kennel cough is not as serious as the other diseases listed above.

Rabies is a deadly viral disease and it is the law in most states that the Rabies vaccine must be given to dogs yearly. The mode of transmission is a bite from an infected animal. The virus affects the brain, causing inability to swallow, subsequent drooling or frothing at the mouth, and the animal will show untypical behavior or aggression. Convulsions, paralysis and death will follow because Rabies is always fatal unless there are injections given immediately after an animal or human has been bitten.

TAKING TEMPERATURE

A healthy puppy has bright eyes and a muscular body and while he is awake will be playful and happy. Should he show signs of lethargy or weakness and you don't know the cause, telephone your vet and take him in for a check. As a preliminary step you can take his temperature so that you will know if he has a fever. Use a rectal thermometer lubricated with petroleum jelly and insert it about three-fourths of an inch into the rectum. Normal temperature is about 101°F, give or take a degree. It is better to err on the side of caution with a puppy and be ready to take him to the vet at any sign of a fever.

Teething

At the age of 4 months your puppy may go off his food quite drastically. He has been a wonderful eater until this time, and you cannot help but be worried. The likely explanation is that he is teething and that his mouth is just plain sore. You can consider giving him soft food for a couple of weeks until the new teeth are in and his mouth is back to normal. Make sure that when his large upper incisors come in that they push out the baby ones. Cavaliers are notorious for retaining these baby teeth, and if they remain for too long they may decay and infect the permanent teeth. Should you notice that the permanent teeth are in and the baby teeth are still there, you can try wiggling the baby teeth and this action may be enough to make them come out. If they are still tight the solution is to take the puppy to the vet to have the baby teeth removed. It is a simple procedure and does not need an anesthetic.

Look at the mouth carefully to see how the new teeth are aligned. To be correct, according to the Cavalier Standard, the upper teeth must overlap the lower in a scissors bite. Sometimes the permanent teeth are undershot, the lower teeth overlapping the upper, and this may be a growth problem which will correct itself by the time the dog is a year or so old. A real problem can occur if the puppy you received from the breeder has an overbite, the upper teeth considerably ahead of the lower. This fault will never correct itself, and when the second teeth come in the large lower incisors can be misaligned enough to impinge on the roof of the mouth making it sore. The only cure for an overbite such as this is to extract the two large lower incisors. Puppies usually return to hearty eating once the adult teeth are established. If a loss of appetite persists for more than a week or two, other causes must be sought with the help of your veterinarian.

Neutering and Spaying

There are advantages for pet owners also in having dogs neutered or spayed. The male dog will not go wandering and watering every tree and bush in the neighborhood to mark his territory and attract females. The smell of urine from a neutered male is much less strong than that of the intact male. If there is a female in season in the area the neutered male will not feel the urge to escape and camp out at her door. Neutering the dog will also avoid testicular cancer or a prostate problem in his later life. The removal of testicles is quite a simple operation for the veterinarian to perform, and the stitches used are self-dissolving. Within a day or two of the operation, the Cavalier will be back to his normal happy self.

There are similar advantages in the case of the spayed female. She will not have to be confined in the house through messy seasons, and you will not have the problem of everybody's mutt trying to jump the fence to invade your yard and in between times peeing on your gate and bushes. Another plus is that the spayed female will be less likely to have breast cancer in later years. The spay operation is a little more complicated than neutering for the male. An incision is made in the abdomen and the ovary and uterus are removed. There are internal and external stitches, and she will have to go back to the veterinarian in ten days to have the few external stitches removed. She should not over exert herself in the first forty-eight hours after the operation, but she will want be normally active after a few days. The only activity that should be discouraged until she has her stitches out is jumping and wrestling or playing hard with other dogs.

Breeding Cavaliers is best left up to professionals in the fancy.

One word of caution is necessary here regarding the possibility of weight gain after neutering and spaying. Watch the waistline of your dog, and cut down the daily intake of food if he is gaining weight on the amount he was getting before he was neutered. There will be accelerated coat growth after neutering or spaying the Cavalier, and the texture of the coat will change, becoming finer and denser. Daily grooming will be more necessary, and you may wish to take your dog to a professional groomer about every six weeks or so to keep the coat under control. Neutering and spaying will *not* change the nature of the Cavalier. He or she will be the same charming, lovable companion you had before the operation.

Inheritable Diseases

The Cavalier is generally a sturdy, healthy dog, but there are genetic tendencies in the breed to particular health problems. All dogs are subject to inheritable diseases, and the Cavalier is no better or worse than other breeds. Though it is ethical for the breeder to inform the prospective pet owner about these diseases there should not be too much emphasis put on them. Reputable breeders put much time, money and effort into lessening the effects of inherited disease in their stock, and most will offer the buyer a year's guarantee from date of birth against any disabling genetic defect. Here follows a list and description of the diseases that can be carried genetically.

MITRAL VALVE DISEASE

MVD is the most serious of the inherited diseases affecting the Cavalier. At the onset of this disease the left mitral valve of the heart begins to degenerate and leak, allowing small amounts of blood to flow the wrong way, causing strain on the heart. As the leak progresses the heart enlarges as it works harder to pump blood. As the disease progresses from this point the dog can go into congestive heart failure. MVD is seldom detected before a dog is a year old, and it usually comes to light at the time the dog goes for annual vaccination and checkup. The vet will hear a murmur on auscultation with a stethoscope though there may be no physical symptoms of heart trouble. A Cavalier may continue on with this slight murmur for many years, and the leak may progress so slowly that he remains without

---

ADVANTAGES OF SPAY/NEUTER

The greatest advantage of spaying (for females) or neutering (for males) your dog is that you are guaranteed your dog will not produce puppies. There are too many puppies already available for too few homes. There are other advantages as well.

Advantages of Spaying

No messy heats.

No "suitors" howling at your windows or waiting in your yard.

Decreased incidences of pyometra (disease of the uterus) and breast cancer.

Advantages of Neutering

Lessens male aggressive and territorial behaviors, but doesn't affect the dog's personality. Behaviors are often owner-induced, so neutering is not the only answer, but it is a good start.

Prevents the need to roam in search of bitches in season.

Decreased incidences of urogenital diseases.

symptoms until he is quite old when degeneration would be expected in any case. In some cases, however, a dog will be detected with a murmur, and will go downhill rapidly, progressing to congestive heart failure at the relatively early age of 7 or 8. A Swedish study of MVD reveals that more than 50 percent of Cavaliers have a murmur detected by stethoscope by the time they are 4 years old. The normal life span of a Cavalier is 10 to 12 years, and it is the aim of breeders to try to produce stock that will be healthy and long-lived.

If you really want lots of puppies, adopt a couple and then buy a pair of slippers! (photo by Norma Moffat)

Environmental factors also play a part in the development of MVD. A dog that is fat and gets little exercise is a prime candidate for the problem. Keeping a Cavalier slim and active will give him the best chance to cope should he be diagnosed with MVD. My first Cavalier, Ollie, who lived to be nearly 15, developed MVD at age 6 and was symptom free until he was more than 12 years old. His remarkable longevity I ascribe entirely to his strong constitution, good nutrition and the fact that he trotted a mile or two every day of his life. The diagnosis of MVD is not a death sentence, and there are a number of helpful drugs that will improve the quality of life for an affected dog. Drugs are usually prescribed when the dog begins to exhibit symptoms such as shortness of breath or coughing, and these can be alleviated with one or a combination of drugs depending upon which symptoms are present.

Veterinarians can supply prescription diets for dogs that have MVD and these are usually fairly low in protein with no salt added.

PATELLAR LUXATION

In ordinary words this orthopedic problem is that of a slipping kneecap (patella). This can occur either through heredity or as the result of an injury. The patella is set in a groove at the front of the femur or thighbone, and in the case of a hereditary problem, can pop out of place if the groove is too shallow. Likewise, an accident or heavy blow at the side of the knee can displace the patella and weaken it so that it may come out of the groove. In the case of accident, once this has occurred it is likely that the kneecap may be easily displaced again. Should there be unexplained occasional limping, or the dog stops now and again to stretch out the affected leg, which causes the kneecap to go back into place, it is possible that the dog has a luxating patella. It is easy for veterinarians to diagnose this condition by manipulation of the leg to see if there is sideways movement of the patella. Veterinary orthopedic surgeons have devised a highly successful operation to correct patellar luxation, which consists of deepening the groove in the femur so that the kneecap will not slip out. The symptoms of this condition may be noticed while the dog is still a puppy and the sooner the operation can be done, the better the results. Later in life the dog may have some arthritis as a result of the operation, but that is better than life with a knee that is crippling and painful. Reputable breeders will test their potential sires and dams and clear them of patellar luxation, and the production of dogs with good solid bone is a first step to correcting the problem. Dogs with delicate legs are much more prone to this kind of problem, and in any case a "chicken-boned" Cavalier is not a pretty sight.

HIP DYSPLASIA

While hip dysplasia does occur occasionally in Cavaliers, it is not as common as patellar luxation. It is much more of a problem in large breeds because puppies of this type put on a lot of bone growth in a very short time. The hip is a ball and socket joint, in normal hips the ball fitting very closely into a nicely rounded socket. In hip dysplasia the socket begins to flatten out and the ball of the head of the femur no longer fits tightly. Laxity in the joint causes more wear and tear on the socket that will eventually grow bone spurs causing a lot of pain for the dog.

Symptoms of Hip Dysplasia

Symptoms of this problem include difficulty in rising after being in one position for some time, leaning forward when sitting so as to take the weight of the body on the front legs and "bunny hopping" with the back legs rather than trotting. A dog may have hip dysplasia and yet show no symptoms for some years. It is only when the disease is quite advanced that the owner may notice limping or the symptoms mentioned above. Anti-inflammatory drugs and painkillers can be prescribed by your vet for a mild condition. If it becomes severe, then an orthopedic surgeon can perform an operation, but this usually requires a long convalescence and is very expensive.

RETINAL DYSPLASIA

The retina of the eye may be compared to a shallow, smooth, round bowl. In dysplasia, the smooth surface has wrinkles or folds to a lesser or greater extent. In a mild case of retinal dysplasia there will be only a few folds, and this is known as the focal type. Where there are many folds, the condition is known as the geographic type. No one can tell you how the dog's sight is affected, and in my experience the dog does not seem to suffer at all from any disability from either grade of retinal dysplasia. If you have a pet Cavalier with retinal dysplasia you may never find out about it. Breeders, however, are very concerned not to knowingly breed this condition into their stock. In other breeds retinal dysplasia has progressed to such a point that dogs suffer retinal detachment and go blind.

When I have a puppy that is going to another breeder as a show prospect I always take it to a veterinary ophthalmologist to be sure the puppy has no retinal dysplasia, or other hereditary eye problem. Retinal dysplasia does not progress as cataracts do, but the danger for the breed is that careless breeding of affected dogs will lead to puppies being born blind with retinal detachment.

CATARACTS

Cataracts are known but very uncommon in the Cavalier, and they may be hereditary or congenital (present from the time of birth). In the congenital type they remain static and do not progress to blindness. Cataracts developing in later life do progress and the end result is blindness, though usually at an advanced age. Dogs so affected can still lead fairly normal lives if they are living continually in a known environment where they know the physical layout of home and yard.

A veterinarian that is familiar with Cavaliers will be sure to examine the eyes carefully.

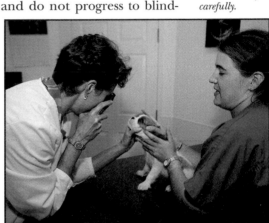

EPILEPSY

The term epilepsy covers all kinds of seizures, and it is difficult if not impossible for a veterinarian to determine if epileptic seizures are the result of an accident as a puppy or if it is heredity. When a dog is having a seizure he will collapse, he may froth at the mouth or his jaw will clench, his legs will move involuntarily and he may lose consciousness for a few moments or even minutes. After the seizure is over, the dog will appear lethargic and when he gets up may seem uncoordinated for a while. Hereditary epilepsy is uncommon in the Cavalier, but is known to occur. It usually begins when the dog is 6 months to a year old, appears without

79

any forewarning and apparently without any particular stress being on the dog at the time. One minute he will be walking happily on the lead and the next on the ground in the throes of a seizure. Fortunately, seizures can be largely controlled by drugs, and many dogs so afflicted can lead a normal life. There is a condition related to epilepsy that may occur in Cavaliers, known as "fly-catching syndrome." The dog looks around and seems to be snapping at flies that are nonexistent. Medication is not needed for this condition since the dog is not disabled in any way, but if it becomes excessive then the same drugs that are used for epilepsy are effective.

Notes on Hereditary Diseases

Now that you have read the section on hereditary diseases, you may think that a breed with these problems is an unhealthy one. Nothing could be further from the truth. All breeds have hereditary disorders, and the Cavalier is about average in this regard. Even crossbreeds can be affected by genetically carried disease, but since no one keeps track of them or reports them, the false impression is given that mutts are healthier than purebreds.

The responsibility for producing the healthiest Cavaliers lies directly on the shoulders of the breeders, and it is in their own interest to try to lessen the effects of hereditary disease in their stock. No reputable breeder wants to sell a puppy, then get a tearful call from a pet owner who has discovered mitral valve disease at an early age or slipping patellas. These conditions may occur in an occasional individual even if the breeder has put heart and soul into the effort to find healthy lines and produce long-lived stock. Over the years a breeder's efforts will eventually pay off as fewer and fewer of their dogs will be affected. It is the pet owner's responsibility when looking for a puppy to ask the right questions of breeders. Do they test their potential sires and dams for hereditary disorders, particularly MVD? Do they continue to test the same sires and dams yearly for MVD? Do they have written confirmation from specialists verifying that they are free from such diseases, and can the prospective pet owner see them?

No matter how hard we try to produce sturdy, healthy dogs, we breeders have to keep in mind that we must consider conformation also. The soundly built, elegant, glamorous royal toy spaniel is what we are endeavoring to produce, and if we manage to come up with a dog totally free of any genetic fault whatever and it does not fit that description, then we have done the breed no service.

Common Ailments
TEETH

Gingivitis and tooth decay are common ailments of the Cavalier. The muzzle is relatively short, compared to a German Shepherd for instance, but they both have the same number of teeth. In consequence the Cavalier's teeth are packed closely together. Brushing daily with a baby toothbrush and toothpaste made specifically for dogs is the best way to avoid infection.

SKIN

Fleas

Of the external parasites, fleas are the most common cause of skin irritation for any dog. They travel to the dog to ingest a blood meal, but they live and lay their eggs in the dog's environment. Though flea baths and body sprays will temporarily rid your Cavalier of fleas, they will recur unless his room, bedding, carpets and baseboards in the vicinity are treated with a premise spray. The safest spray is one that uses natural pyrethrin because it is least toxic to the dog. As with ear health, acting upon the very first sign of a problem is the key to getting rid of fleas. If he has picked up a flea or two you will see little specks of black on the skin near the tail in particular. Those specks of black are flea droppings and the sure sign that your pet has unwelcome visitors.

In the past few years new and effective chemical treatments have been developed to combat fleas. One works internally so that when the flea bites the dog the flea cannot reproduce, thus eliminating any more infestation. The other works externally, a spot of liquid being applied to the dog's back. The liquid spreads itself over the dog's entire skin in time and will kill all fleas. Both these remedies are available only from a veterinarian, and so far have been proven safe. If your dog is only bothered occasionally with a flea or two, the flea bath and treatment of the premises when necessary is the natural way to go, but if you live in a warm climate and fleas are a continuing problem, then the monthly treatments may be preferable. Some fleas can also carry tapeworm, and should your dog ingest one of infected fleas he will soon have his very own parasite. For certain sensitive dogs flea allergy dermatitis, appearing as crusted areas of skin with considerable loss of hair around the tail area, will be the result of only a few bites, and this condition will require veterinary care.

FLEAS AND TICKS

There are so many safe, effective products available now to combat fleas and ticks that—thankfully— these pests are less of a problem. Prevention is key, however. Ask your veterinarian about starting your puppy on a flea/tick repellent right away. With this, regular grooming and environmental controls, your dog and your home should stay pest-free. Without this attention, you risk infesting your dog and your home, and you're in for an ugly and costly battle to clear up the problem.

Ticks

Infestation with the brown dog tick is less common than flea infestation, but in southern areas in particular, ticks are more plentiful. All that is needed is to watch out for them when grooming.

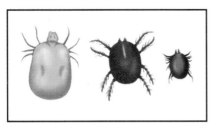

Three types of ticks (l-r): the wood tick, brown dog tick and deer tick.

They must be removed with tweezers, and since the tick head is buried under the dog's skin it must be done so that head comes away with the tick's body. My method is to take a drop of pure tea tree oil and dab it on the tick. The shock will cause him to almost let go, then you can get a firm grip on the body and give a sharp pull. When the tick is out, put on another drop of tea tree oil and work it into the skin.

A hazard to dogs and humans alike is the deer tick that can carry Lyme disease. Dogs living in the countryside are more liable to pick up a deer tick. If your dog picks up a tick and it is gray rather than brown, it is likely to be a deer tick. Symptoms of Lyme disease begin with a rash that extends in a circle from the area of the bite.

Following that first sign the dog may exhibit fever, staggering, weakness and subsequent swelling of the joints. Lyme disease can end in severe arthritis and heart problems.

Mites

There are several kinds of mites that can infest the skin, and the most common among Cavaliers is the Cheyletiella mange mite, known as walking dandruff. They spend their lives on their host and generally do not get into the surrounding environment as fleas do. It is a good idea, nevertheless, to change the dog's bedding if he has to be treated for mite infection.

Use tweezers to remove ticks from your dog.

Cheyletiella mites burrow into the skin to lay their eggs. There is intense itching of the skin and the dog will chew himself trying to get rid of the itch. When the mites hatch out, a flake of skin comes off and this is the dandruff that the pet owner can see. Apart from the apparent skin flakes, the coat will become thin and lose its luster. The mite itself cannot be seen with the naked eye, but can be detected with the veterinarian's microscope. If the dog is itching and there is no apparent reason, then a visit to the vet is in order to determine the cause. He will take a skin scraping from an area most likely to be affected to see if mites are present. A bath with flea shampoo once a week for three weeks should rid the dog of mites, but should they persist, and they are very tenacious, the vet can treat the dog with an insecticidal dip, which is much more toxic than the shampoo method. A new treatment for cheyletiella is injection with ivermectin, the same ingredient that is the basis of heartworm medication.

Sarcoptic and demodectic mange are of a more serious nature and can only be diagnosed by a professional. At any sign of continual scratching, loss of hair around the eyes or lesions on the skin, the dog should be seen by the veterinarian without delay.

INTERNAL PARASITES

Roundworms are the worms most commonly found in young puppies. In the case of whelps still in the nest, they are born with worms in their intestines that have formed there after traveling from an encysted site in the mother's body. Occasionally, adults may also be affected though this is less common. The worms can also be transmitted through contact with the feces of other animals. Part of the dog's nature is to sniff at other animals'

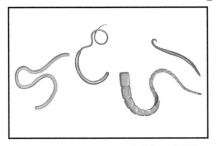

Common internal parasites (l-r): roundworm, whipworm, tapeworm and hookworm.

feces, and such a contact is all that is needed to begin an infestation of roundworm. Symptoms are loss of weight, a distended belly and staring dry coat.

Hookworms are parasites of the small intestine. They hook themselves into the intestine and begin to suck blood. They move from one site to another in the intestine, and when they do so the site they leave will continue to bleed. Symptoms include diarrhea with streaks of dark blood in it. Dogs will become debilitated and anemic from an infestation of hookworm. It is passed along through eggs in the feces, or from the soil where feces have been. Soil-borne eggs of the hookworm are a hazard to humans as well as dogs. When a person or dog walks over the hatched eggs the worms can enter the body by burrowing through the skin of the feet. From this location they will migrate to the small intestine of the host and attach themselves, beginning another cycle of infestation.

Whipworms are parasites that feed on blood from the wall of the lower intestine. Eggs are passed through the feces and into the soil. The eggs are very hardy and can live for years in the soil until they are picked up by a dog as he digs and sniffs the ground, ingesting the eggs and beginning the cycle again. Symptoms include anemia caused by bloody diarrhea, loss of weight and general debilitation.

Tapeworms are very long segmented worms that feed on fluids from the intestinal wall. They shed old segments into the feces and onto the area surrounding the anus. See below for further information on the control of this worm.

Heartworms are carried by an intermediate host, the mosquito. It bites an infected dog and ingests heartworm microfilariae which are present in the dog's blood. When the mosquito bites another dog, a little of the infected blood is introduced and the heartworm cycle begins. A dog whose infections goes undetected will deveop large adult worms which will clog the heart, and death is the end result. Medication for prevention of heartworm is essential in nearly all areas of the United States. Prevention of heartworm is simple; a pill given once a month will kill any micro-filariae in the blood. A dog that already has worms in the heart can be treated with drugs that are basically poisons but even if the worms are dislodged by chemical means, the dog's heart will be weak for life.

In the case of pets that are cared for on a regular basis by a veterinarian, round, hook and whipworms are no longer the threat they were in the past. Heartworm pills also include chemicals that will eliminate all these worms. Tapeworm, however, is not affected by this medication, and when grooming the dog the pet owner should take a good look at the Cavalier's anus and surrounding hair for any sign of this parasite. If tapeworm is present, you will see what looks like little white or brownish grains of rice sticking to the hair. Poop-scooping right after a dog defecates may reveal fresh white moving segments of tapeworm in the feces. The most common way a dog picks up tapeworm is through chewing at himself and ingesting an infected flea. Treatment of tapeworm is simple and easy, one pill, usually Droncit, prescribed by your veterinarian.

Any dog will take it down easily coated in cream cheese or peanut butter. The chemical in the pill will dissolve the skin of the tapeworm, and it will be totally digested and eliminated by the dog.

Those Cavaliers who live in the country with all kinds of wildlife that can transmit parasites need to be watched carefully for poor condition of coat, lethargy and haggard appearance that would indicate worms, and physical evidence of tapeworm.

Patent Worm Remedies

Never buy patent worm remedies that are for sale in the pet-supply store or supermarket. In the first place, it is unnecessary medication if the dog does not need it, and secondly the medication may be incorrect for the type of worm the dog has. Taking a stool sample to your veterinarian for analysis once every six months is good insurance against worms of any kind.

ANAL GLANDS

I have commented on the breed trait of "scooting" in Chapter 3. Even young puppies will exhibit this behavior on an occasional basis. The difference between this habit and scooting because of full or impacted anal glands is in the frequency with which it occurs. There is an operation that can be done to remove the glands if the problem is chronic, but this is a last resort as it is a delicate and expensive operation, and it is possible that the dog can be left incontinent.

VOMITING

Vomiting is a natural reaction of the Cavalier when his stomach is irritated for any reason. In fact, dogs will deliberately go out and eat types of coarse grass that will cause vomiting. The time to be concerned about vomiting is if the dog vomits up his meals on a regular basis or if the vomit has a foul odor. Another reason for being concerned is that continued vomiting may indicate a blockage of the bowel. In these cases, a visit to the veterinarian is in order to determine the cause of the problem.

Cavaliers may get stomach upsets from a change of food, change of water when traveling or because they have picked up something tainted from the ground and swallowed it. As long as the diarrhea is not bloody and foul and stops within a few hours, there should be no more problems. Diarrhea that continues past this time may be more serious in origin and should be treated by a veterinarian.

First Aid Kit

A first aid kit is easily assembled, and should be kept in the home or carried in the car when your Cavalier travels with you. It is a good idea to keep the contents in a clear plastic box so that you can see what you want at a glance. I keep the following items in my emergency kit:

- Cotton gauze pads to cover wounds, or to apply pressure to prevent bleeding.

- Cotton gauze bandage rolls to hold pads in place. A length of bandage roll makes a good muzzle should the dog be in an accident, in pain and likely to bite. Gauze bandage doubled can be used as a tourniquet to slow bleeding in case of accident to legs or tail.

- Two rolls of adhesive tape, one narrow to secure bandages, one wide which can be applied over bandage or a rolled newspaper to make a temporary splint for a strained or broken limb.

 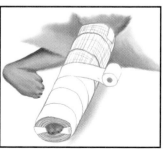

Make a temporary splint by wrapping the leg in firm casing, then bandaging it.

- Scissors for cutting bandages and to clip around wounds before dressing.

- Tweezers for pulling out thorns or small foreign objects from the skin.

- Cotton balls for swabbing out wounds.

- Hydrogen peroxide as a general cleaning agent for wounds.

- Saline solution to wash injured eyes.

- Eye bath or egg cup for applying saline solution.

- Syringe for squirting liquids or medication down the throat.

- Soothing medicated skin ointment for minor wounds.

- Medicated eye ointment such as polysporin for minor eye injury.

- Buffered aspirin to alleviate pain.

- Diarrhea remedy such as neo atrapec or Pepto Bismol.

- Activated charcoal to absorb poison.

- Child's crib blanket for wrapping or warming an injured dog.

- Small flashlight for emergencies outside at night and to look down a dog's throat for obstructions.

In the first aid box should also be your veterinarian's telephone number and after hours emergency number, since is easy in the panic of the moment to be unable to keep it in your memory.

WHEN TO CALL THE VETERINARIAN

In any emergency situation, you should call your veterinarian immediately. Try to stay calm when you call, and give the vet or the assistant as much information as possible before you leave for the clinic. That way, the staff will be able to take immediate, specific action when you arrive. Emergencies include:

- Bleeding or deep wounds

- Hyperthermia (overheating)

- Shock

- Dehydration

- Abdominal pain

- Burns

- Fits

- Unconsciousness

- Broken bones

- Paralysis

Call your veterinarian if you suspect any health troubles.

What to Do in an Emergency
DOG BITES

A Cavalier is a sociable soul, and if not watched will run happily to any person with a dog in the park to make their acquaintance. Trouble can often result when the other dog, following a guard instinct, takes exception to this carefree visitor and bites him as a result. Such wounds are usually of the puncture type, and can be easily dealt with. First, press on the puncture wound from underneath so that it will bleed a little to expel bacteria that may have got into the wound with the teeth. Next, take a cotton pad and soak the wound well with hydrogen peroxide. Puncture wounds may swell and be painful but they seldom need stitches. There is no rush, but a visit to the veterinarian within twelve to twenty-four hours is in order so that he can prescribe an antibiotic to avoid any infection. Should your dog be bitten and held on to before you can rescue him, there may be a tear in the skin as well as puncture wounds. If there is considerable bleeding apply hand pressure to the wound to slow it. Flush the wound as soon as you can with hydrogen peroxide and get to a veterinarian right away because stitches may be necessary.

CHOKING

All kinds of objects can get stuck in your dog's throat—small balls, sticks or pieces of soft plastic toys, for example. Symptoms are gagging and coughing as the dog tries to dislodge the object and he will be frantic. If you have another person handy, get them to hold the dog still. Open his mouth to see if you can see the object and hook it out with your finger. If you cannot hook it out, hold the dog slanting

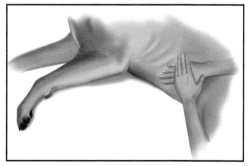

Applying abdominal thrusts can save a choking dog.

downwards and hit him sharply between the shoulders near the neck to see if it will pop out. If this does not work you can try laying the dog on his side and compressing sharply just behind the ribs. The hope is that air will be forced out of the lungs and the object with it.

HEATSTROKE

The most common cause of heatstroke is a dog left in a car in the summer. The symptoms of heatstroke are rapid panting, the appearance of thick bubbling saliva, staggering and collapse. Wet the dog thoroughly as soon as you possibly can, or put him in a bath of cool water. Don't use ice in the water because it is too much of a shock to the system. He may be too weak to drink voluntarily, but you can squirt small amounts of water from a syringe down his throat at frequent intervals. He may be quite weak from the shock to his system afterwards, and then it is time to dry him well with a towel, wrap him in a blanket and keep him in a cool place for the next few hours.

POISON ALERT

If your dog has ingested a potentially poisonous substance, waste no time. Call the National Animal Poison Control Center hot line:

(800) 548-2423 ($30 per case)

or

(900) 680-0000
($20 first five minutes; $2.95 each additional minute)

HYPOTHERMIA

It is less usual for a Cavalier to suffer from hypothermia, but it can happen as a result of being in very cold water, or being outside in a northern winter too long without physical activity to keep the body warm. Symptoms of hypothermia include violent shivering, a belly that will feel cold to the touch, and a dog that will only be able to move very slowly. If he is wet, dry him off as best you can. Wrap him in a towel and cuddle him next to your own body underneath your sweater. If he is dry you can just put him under the sweater to begin warming. The best treatment for hypothermia is gradual, not quick, warming, and body heat will do it nicely until you can get him indoors. Once inside, wrap him in a blanket to conserve his own body heat, and put him in his own bed. Place large plastic soda pop bottles filled with warm water on each side of him and replenish as needed.

ELECTRIC SHOCK

Puppies are particularly vulnerable to this type of injury because they want to find out about the world with their teeth. Electrical outlets in the home are usually near the floor and lamps are always left plugged in. A chewing puppy can get a serious shock if he is not discovered before his teeth contact the live wire in the cord, and the shock can be so severe that he can die. If he is not breathing, try artificial respiration as described for major trauma. Wrap him warmly and take him directly to the veterinarian for anti-shock treatment.

MAJOR TRAUMA

After an accident, the first concerns should be to stop bleeding as much as possible.

Bleeding from a limb can be slowed in an emergency by using a tourniquet above the wound. A belt or a tie can be used for this purpose, but the tourniquet must be loosened every ten minutes in order to keep the circulation in the limb going. If bleeding from a body wound, cover with the cleanest cloth you have available and apply pressure. If the dog is conscious and snapping because of pain, a muzzle can be made out of a tie, scarf or belt. Wind it round the muzzle and then around the back of the head and secure it. To transport the dog for veterinary help, don't pick him up by the body. Roll him into some sort of sling—your jacket or a blanket for instance—pull it taut and carry him as on a stretcher.

Use a scarf or old hose to make a temporary muzzle, as shown.

POISONS

Common poisons around the home and yard include the following: Antifreeze, chocolate, cleaning solvents, disinfectants, houseplants, insecticides, slug bait,

*Keep all poten-
tial poisons out
of your curious
Cavalier's
reach.*

mouse or rat poison, pine oil cleaners, soaps and detergents. Symptoms of poisoning include vomiting, convulsions, lack of coordination and collapse. If you suspect poisoning, get to the veterinarian as quickly as possible because some poisons are fast acting.

As Your Cavalier Ages

LIFE SPAN

The normal life span of a Cavalier is about 10 to 12 years. The rule of thumb with dog breeds is that the smaller the breed, the longer the life span, but this does not apply to the Cavalier as it does to some of the other toy breeds who may live until they are 16 years old. A Cavalier may have excellent health all his life, but it is likely that for the last year or two of it he will have heart disease, and his ultimate death will be from this cause. The hearts of all breeds deteriorate as they age; it is a normal process. The Cavalier, however, has a genetic tendency to mitral valve disease, and this puts him more at risk.

KEEPING ACTIVE

By the time a Cavalier is 8 years old he may be considered a senior citizen. Every effort should be made to keep him active, and not to let him turn into a couch potato. He will want to rest more often, it is true, but his daily walk is even more essential now to keep him limber and his internal organs in good condition. If he is left to sleep away the day, his general condition will deteriorate and he will become fat and unhealthy.

VETERINARY CARE

A young dog in good health needs to go to the vet for a checkup only once a year. It is a good idea to go twice yearly with an older dog so that if there is any health problem it can be caught in the early stages and dealt with. Possible ailments of the older Cavalier include heart disease, cancer, diabetes, kidney or liver disease.

FEEDING THE OLDER CAVALIER

A good-quality food designed for seniors is all that is needed for the dog that is still in good health, but you must watch quantities carefully since his metabolism is slower and he may put on weight. If he is not as interested in his food as he formerly was, give him two small meals a day with a little extra meat to spark his appetite. Should your veterinarian diagnose a heart or kidney condition, or should your dog be getting fat on the food you are using, his or her office will carry special diets designed for these problems. I supplement my older dogs with anti-oxidants vitamins E and C along with their regular ration of dry food, raw meat and pureed raw vegetables. Continue to give him treats that are hard and chewy to stimulate the teeth and gums.

A well-cared-for Cavalier can live beyond his expected years—the one shown here is a sprightly 15 years old!

Even though the dog is eating normally, combined with excessive thirst may be signs of diabetes, and any weight loss without a ready explanation should be checked out by a visit to the veterinarian.

A NOTE ABOUT OLD AGE IN GENERAL

It may seem from the previous text that the Cavalier is a hotbed of problems in old age. The ailments listed above apply to all older dogs, not just Cavaliers. In fact, the well-cared-for older Cavalier is usually a sturdy, perfectly healthy dog for all but a short period towards the end of his life.

SAYING GOODBYE TO A FAITHFUL FRIEND

No matter how long your beloved Cavalier lives, it will never be long enough to suit you. Dog lives are all too short, and it seems that it is difficult to resign ourselves to the fact that the puppy we brought home and cherished as a dear member of the family has become old and infirm. The best possible end for your Cavalier is that he passes away from plain old age peacefully in his sleep, but the time may come when a terminal illness is diagnosed, he is in pain and decisions must be made. A consultation with your veterinarian will help you to decide whether to continue active treatment or whether palliative care with pain-killing drugs will be the option. Your Cavalier has given you the very best that is in him: affection, faithfulness, emotional support in times of trouble and always with that effervescent sparkling spirit that is the hallmark of the true Cavalier. It is now your turn to support him as best you can in his final days. Eventually, there will be a choice to be made as to whether euthanasia would be the kindest option.

The grieving process after the loss of your Cavalier is very like that for a person. You will wonder how you could feel so devastated by the loss of a mere animal, but people who own Cavaliers know that they are like little people in dog clothing. They are in tune with your moods, always excellent company and that is what makes them wonderful pets.

Your Happy, Healthy Pet

Your Dog's Name _____

Name on Your Dog's Pedigree (if your dog has one) _____

_____

Where Your Dog Came From _____

_____

Your Dog's Birthday _____

Your Dog's Veterinarian

    Name _____

    Address _____

    Phone Number_____

    Emergency Number_____

Your Dog's Health

    Vaccines

        type _____ date given _____

        type _____ date given _____

        type _____ date given _____

        type _____ date given _____

    Heartworm

        date tested _____ type used_____ start date _____

Your Dog's License Number_____

Groomer's Name and Number _____

Dogsitter/Walker's Name and Number_____

Awards Your Dog Has Won

    Award _____ date earned _____

    Award _____ date earned _____

part three

Enjoying
your
Dog

chapter 8

Basic
Training

by Ian Dunbar, Ph.D., MRCVS

Training is the jewel in the crown—the most important aspect of doggy husbandry. There is no more important variable influencing dog behavior and temperament than the dog's education: A well-trained, well-behaved and good-natured puppydog is always a joy to live with, but an untrained and uncivilized dog can be a perpetual nightmare. Moreover, deny the dog an education and she will not have the opportunity to fulfill her own canine potential; neither will she have the ability to communicate effectively with her human companions.

Luckily, modern psychological training methods are easy, efficient, effective and, above all, considerably dog-friendly and user-friendly.

98

Doggy education is as simple as it is enjoyable. But before you can have a good time play-training with your new dog, you have to learn what to do and how to do it. There is no bigger variable influencing the success of dog training than the *owner's* experience and expertise. *Before you embark on the dog's education, you must first educate yourself.*

Basic Training for Owners

Ideally, basic owner training should begin well *before* you select your dog. Find out all you can about your chosen breed first, then master rudimentary training and handling skills. If you already have your puppy-dog, owner training is a dire emergency—the clock is ticking! Especially for puppies, the first few weeks at home are the most important and influential days in the dog's life. Indeed, the cause of most adolescent and adult problems may be traced back to the initial days the pup explores her new home. This is the time to establish the *status quo*—to teach the puppydog how you would like her to behave and so prevent otherwise quite predictable problems.

In addition to consulting breeders and breed books such as this one (which understandably have a positive breed bias), seek out as many pet owners with your breed as you can find. Good points are obvious. What you want to find out are the breed-specific *problems,* so you can nip them in the bud. In particular, you should talk to owners with *adolescent* dogs and make a list of all anticipated problems. Most important, *test drive* at least half a dozen adolescent and adult dogs of your breed yourself. An 8-week-old puppy is deceptively easy to handle, but she will acquire adult size, speed and strength in just four months, so you should learn now what to prepare for.

Puppy and pet dog training classes offer a convenient venue to locate pet owners and observe dogs in action. For a list of suitable trainers in your area, contact the Association of Pet Dog Trainers (see chapter 13). You may also begin your basic owner training by observing

other owners in class. Watch as many classes and test
drive as many dogs as possible. Select an upbeat, dog-
friendly, people-friendly, fun-and-games, puppydog pet
training class to learn the ropes. Also, watch training
videos and read training books. You must find out what
to do and how to do it *before* you have to do it.

Principles of Training

Most people think training comprises teaching the dog
to do things such as sit, speak and roll over, but even a
4-week-old pup knows how to do these things already.
Instead, the first step in training involves teaching
the dog human words for each dog behavior and activity and for each aspect of the dog's environment. That
way you, the owner, can more easily participate in the
dog's domestic education by directing her to perform
specific actions appropriately, that is, at the right time,
in the right place and so on. Training opens communication channels, enabling an educated dog to at least
understand her owner's requests.

In addition to teaching a dog *what* we want her to
do, it is also necessary to teach her *why* she should do
what we ask. Indeed, 95 percent of training revolves
around motivating the dog *to want to do* what we want.
Dogs often understand what their owners want; they
just don't see the point of doing it—especially when
the owner's repetitively boring and seemingly senseless
instructions are totally at odds with much more press-
ing and exciting doggy distractions. It is not so much
the dog that is being stubborn or dominant; rather, it
is the owner who has failed to acknowledge the dog's
needs and feelings and to approach training from the
dog's point of view.

THE MEANING OF INSTRUCTIONS

The secret to successful training is learning how to use
training lures to predict or prompt specific behaviors—
to coax the dog to do what you want *when* you want.
Any highly valued object (such as a treat or toy) may be
used as a lure, which the dog will follow with her eyes

and nose. Moving the lure in specific ways entices the dog to move her nose, head and entire body in specific ways. In fact, by learning the art of manipulating various lures, it is possible to teach the dog to assume virtually any body position and perform any action. Once you have control over the expression of the dog's behaviors and can elicit any body position or behavior at will, you can easily teach the dog to perform on request.

Teach your dog words for each activity she needs to know, like down.

Tell your dog what you want her to do, use a lure to entice her to respond correctly, then profusely praise and maybe reward her once she performs the desired action. For example, verbally request "Tina, sit!" while you move a squeaky toy upwards and backwards over the dog's muzzle (lure-movement and hand signal), smile knowingly as she looks up (to follow the lure) and sits down (as a result of canine anatomical engineering), then praise her to distraction ("Gooood Tina!"). Squeak the toy, offer a training treat and give your dog and yourself a pat on the back.

Being able to elicit desired responses over and over enables the owner to reward the dog over and over. Consequently, the dog begins to think training is fun. For example, the more the dog is rewarded for sitting, the more she enjoys sitting. Eventually the dog comes

101

Enjoying Your Dog

to realize that, whereas most sitting is appreciated, sitting immediately upon request usually prompts especially enthusiastic praise and a slew of high-level rewards. The dog begins to sit on cue much of the time, showing that she is starting to grasp the meaning of the owner's verbal request and hand signal.

WHY COMPLY?

Most dogs enjoy initial lure-reward training and are only too happy to comply with their owners' wishes. Unfortunately, repetitive drilling without appreciative feedback tends to diminish the dog's enthusiasm until she eventually fails to see the point of complying anymore. Moreover, as the dog approaches adolescence she becomes more easily distracted as she develops other interests. Lengthy sessions with repetitive exercises tend to bore and demotivate both parties. If it's not fun, the owner doesn't do it and neither does the dog.

Integrate training into your dog's life: The greater number of training sessions each day and the *shorter* they are, the more willingly compliant your dog will

become. Make sure to have a short (just a few seconds) training interlude before every enjoyable canine activity. For example, ask your dog to sit to greet people, to sit before you throw her Frisbee and to sit for her supper. Really, sitting is no different from a canine "Please."

To train your dog, you need gentle hands, a loving heart and a good attitude.

Also, include numerous short training interludes during every enjoyable canine pastime, for example, when playing with the dog or when she is running in the park. In this fashion, doggy distractions may be effectively converted into rewards for training. Just as all games have rules, fun becomes training . . . and training becomes fun.

Eventually, rewards actually become unnecessary to continue motivating your dog. If trained with consideration and kindness, performing the desired behaviors will become self-rewarding and, in a sense, your dog will motivate herself. Just as it is not necessary to reward a human companion during an enjoyable walk in the park, or following a game of tennis, it is hardly necessary to reward our best friend—the dog—for walking by our side or while playing fetch. Human company during enjoyable activities is reward enough for most dogs.

Even though your dog has become self-motivating, it's still good to praise and pet her a lot and offer rewards once in a while, especially for a good job well done. And if for no other reason, praising and rewarding others is good for the human heart.

PUNISHMENT

Without a doubt, lure-reward training is by far the best way to teach: Entice your dog to do what you want and then reward her for doing so. Unfortunately, a human shortcoming is to take the good for granted and to moan and groan at the bad. Specifically, the dog's many good behaviors are ignored while the owner focuses on punishing the dog for making mistakes. In extreme cases, instruction is *limited* to punishing mistakes made by a trainee dog, child, employee or husband, even though it has been proven punishment training is notoriously inefficient and ineffective and is decidedly unfriendly and combative. It teaches the dog that training is a drag, almost as quickly as it teaches the dog to dislike her trainer. Why treat our best friends like our worst enemies?

Punishment training is also much more laborious and time consuming. Whereas it takes only a finite amount of time to teach a dog what to chew, for example, it takes much, much longer to punish the dog for each and every mistake. Remember, *there is only one right way!* So why not teach that right way from the outset?!

To make matters worse, punishment training causes severe lapses in the dog's reliability. Since it is obviously impossible to punish the dog each and every time she misbehaves, the dog quickly learns to distinguish between those times when she must comply (so as to avoid impending punishment) and those times when she need not comply, because punishment is impossible. Such times include when the dog is off leash and 6 feet away, when the owner is otherwise engaged (talking to a friend, watching television, taking a shower, tending to the baby or chatting on the telephone) or when the dog is left at home alone.

Instances of misbehavior will be numerous when the owner is away, because even when the dog complied in the owner's looming presence, she did so unwillingly. The dog was forced to act against her will, rather than molding her will to want to please. Hence, when the owner is absent, not only does the dog know she need not comply, she simply does not want to. Again, the trainee is not a stubborn vindictive beast, but rather the trainer has failed to teach. Punishment training invariably creates unpredictable Jekyll and Hyde behavior.

Trainer's Tools

Many training books extol the virtues of a vast array of training paraphernalia and electronic and metallic gizmos, most of which are designed for canine restraint, correction and punishment, rather than for actual facilitation of doggy education. In reality, most effective training tools are not found in stores; they come from within ourselves. In addition to a willing dog, all you really need is a functional human brain, gentle hands, a loving heart and a good attitude.

In terms of equipment, all dogs do require a quality buckle collar to sport dog tags and to attach the leash (for safety and to comply with local leash laws). Hollow chew toys (like Kongs or sterilized longbones) and a dog bed or collapsible crate are musts for housetraining. Three additional tools are required:

1. specific lures (training treats and toys) to predict and prompt specific desired behaviors;

2. rewards (praise, affection, training treats and toys) to reinforce for the dog what a lot of fun it all is; and

3. knowledge—how to convert the dog's favorite activities and games (potential distractions to training) into "life-rewards," which may be employed to facilitate training.

The most powerful of these is *knowledge*. Education is the key! Watch training classes, participate in training classes, watch videos, read books, enjoy play-training with your dog and then your dog will say "Please," and your dog will say "Thank you!"

Housetraining

If dogs were left to their own devices, certainly they would chew, dig and bark for entertainment and then no doubt highlight a few areas of their living space with sprinkles of urine, in much the same way we decorate by hanging pictures. Consequently, when we ask a dog to live with us, we must teach her *where* she may dig, *where* she may perform her toilet duties, *what* she may chew and *when* she may bark. After all, when left at home alone for many hours, we cannot expect the dog to amuse herself by completing crosswords or watching the soaps on TV!

Also, it would be decidedly unfair to keep the house rules a secret from the dog, and then get angry and punish the poor critter for inevitably transgressing rules she did not even know existed. Remember: Without adequate education and guidance, the dog will be forced to establish her own rules—doggy rules—and most probably will be at odds with the owner's view of domestic living.

Since most problems develop during the first few days the dog is at home, prospective dog owners must be certain they are quite clear about the principles of housetraining *before* they get a dog. Early misbehaviors quickly become established as the *status quo*—

becoming firmly entrenched as hard-to-break bad
habits, which set the precedent for years to come.
Make sure to teach your dog good habits right from
the start. Good habits are just as hard to break as bad
ones!

Ideally, when a new dog comes home, try to arrange
for someone to be present as much as possible during
the first few days (for adult dogs) or weeks for puppies.
With only a little forethought, it is surprisingly easy to
find a puppy sitter, such as a retired person, who would
be willing to eat from your refrigerator and watch your
television while keeping an eye on the newcomer to
encourage the dog to play with chew toys and to ensure
she goes outside on a regular basis.

POTTY TRAINING

To teach the dog where to relieve herself:

1. never let her make a single mistake;

2. let her know where you want her to go; and

3. handsomely reward her for doing so:
   "GOOOOOOOD DOG!!!" liver treat, liver treat,
   liver treat!

Preventing Mistakes

A single mistake is a training disaster, since it heralds
many more in future weeks. And each time the dog
soils the house, this further reinforces the dog's un-
fortunate preference for an indoor, carpeted toilet.
*Do not let an unhousetrained dog have full run of the
house.*

When you are away from home, or cannot pay full attention, confine the dog to an area where elimination is
appropriate, such as an outdoor run or, better still, a
small, comfortable indoor kennel with access to an outdoor run. When confined in this manner, most dogs
will naturally housetrain themselves.

If that's not possible, confine the dog to an area, such
as a utility room, kitchen, basement or garage, where

elimination may not be desired in the long run but as an interim measure it is certainly preferable to doing it all around the house. Use newspaper to cover the floor of the dog's day room. The newspaper may be used to soak up the urine and to wrap up and dispose of the feces. Once your dog develops a preferred spot for eliminating, it is only necessary to cover that part of the floor with newspaper. The smaller papered area may then be moved (only a little each day) towards the door to the outside. Thus the dog will develop the tendency to go to the door when she needs to relieve herself.

Never confinc an unhousetrained dog to a crate for long periods. Doing so would force the dog to soil the crate and ruin its usefulness as an aid for housetraining (see the following discussion).

Teaching Where

In order to teach your dog where you would like her to do her business, you have to be there to direct the proceedings—an obvious, yet often neglected, fact of life. In order to be there to teach the dog *where* to go, you need to know *when* she needs to go. Indeed, the success of housetraining depends on the owner's ability to predict these times. Certainly, a regular feeding schedule will facilitate prediction somewhat, but there is nothing like "loading the deck" and influencing the timing of the outcome yourself!

Whenever you are at home, make sure the dog is under constant supervision and/or confined to a small

The first few weeks at home are the most important and influential in your dog's life.

area. If already well trained, simply instruct the dog to lie down in her bed or basket. Alternatively, confine the dog to a crate (doggy den) or tie-down (a short, 18-inch lead that can be clipped to an eye hook in the baseboard near her bed). Short-term close confinement strongly inhibits urination and defecation, since the dog does not want to soil her sleeping area. Thus, when you release the puppydog each hour, she will definitely need to urinate immediately and defecate every third or fourth hour. Keep the dog confined to her doggy den and take her to her intended toilet area each hour, every hour and on the hour.

When taking your dog outside, instruct her to sit quietly before opening the door—she will soon learn to sit by the door when she needs to go out!

Teaching Why

Being able to predict when the dog needs to go enables the owner to be on the spot to praise and reward the dog. Each hour, hurry the dog to the intended toilet area in the yard, issue the appropriate instruction ("Go pee!" or "Go poop!"), then give the dog three to four minutes to produce. Praise and offer a couple of training treats when successful. The treats are important because many people fail to praise their dogs with feeling . . . and housetraining is hardly the time for understatement. So either loosen up and enthusiastically praise that dog: "Wuzzzer-wuzzer-wuzzer, hoooser good wuffer den? Hoooo went pee for Daddy?" Or say "Good dog!" as best you can and offer the treats for effect.

Following elimination is an ideal time for a spot of play-training in the yard or house. Also, an empty dog may be allowed greater freedom around the house for the next half hour or so, just as long as you keep an eye out to make sure she does not get into other kinds of mischief. If you are preoccupied and cannot pay full attention, confine the dog to her doggy den once more to enjoy a peaceful snooze or to play with her many chew toys.

If your dog does not eliminate within the allotted time outside—no biggie! Back to her doggy den, and then try again after another hour.

As I own large dogs, I always feel more relaxed walking an empty dog, knowing that I will not need to finish our stroll weighted down with bags of feces!

Beware of falling into the trap of walking the dog to get her to eliminate. The good ol' dog walk is such an enormous highlight in the dog's life that it represents the single biggest potential reward in domestic dogdom. However, when in a hurry, or during inclement weather, many owners abruptly terminate the walk the moment the dog has done her business. This, in effect, severely punishes the dog for doing the right thing, in the right place at the right time. Consequently, many dogs become strongly inhibited from eliminating outdoors because they know it will signal an abrupt end to an otherwise thoroughly enjoyable walk.

Instead, instruct the dog to relieve herself in the yard prior to going for a walk. If you follow the above instructions, most dogs soon learn to eliminate on cue. As soon as the dog eliminates, praise (and offer a treat or two)—"Good dog! Let's go walkies!" Use the walk as a reward for eliminating in the yard. If the dog does not go, put her back in her doggy den and think about a walk later on. You will find with a "No feces—no walk" policy, your dog will become one of the fastest defecators in the business.

If you do not have a backyard, instruct the dog to eliminate right outside your front door prior to the walk. Not only will this facilitate clean up and disposal of the feces in your own trash can but, also, the walk may again be used as a colossal reward.

CHEWING AND BARKING

Short-term close confinement also teaches the dog that occasional quiet moments are a reality of domestic living. Your puppydog is extremely impressionable during her first few weeks at home. Regular confinement at this time soon exerts a calming influence over the dog's personality. Remember, once the dog is housetrained and calmer, there will be a whole lifetime ahead for the dog to enjoy full run of the house and garden. On the other hand, by letting the newcomer have unrestricted access to the entire household and allowing her to run willy-nilly, she will most certainly develop a bunch of behavior problems in short order, no doubt necessitating confinement later in life. It would not be fair to remedially restrain and confine a dog you have trained, through neglect, to run free.

When confining the dog, make sure she always has an impressive array of suitable chew toys. Kongs and sterilized longbones (both readily available from pet stores) make the best chew toys, since they are hollow and may be stuffed with treats to heighten the dog's interest. For example, by stuffing the little hole at the top of a Kong with a small piece of freeze-dried liver, the dog will not want to leave it alone.

Remember, treats do not have to be junk food and they certainly should not represent extra calories. Rather, treats should be part of each dog's regular daily diet: Some food may be served in the dog's bowl for breakfast and dinner, some food may be used as training treats, and some food may be used for stuffing chew toys. I regularly stuff my dogs' many Kongs with different shaped biscuits and kibble.

Make sure your puppy has suitable chew toys.

The kibble seems to fall out fairly easily, as do the oval-shaped biscuits, thus rewarding the dog instantaneously for checking out the chew toys. The bone-shaped biscuits fall out after a while, rewarding the dog for worrying at the chew toy. But the triangular biscuits never come out. They remain inside the Kong as lures, maintaining the dog's fascination with her chew toy. To further focus the dog's interest, I always make sure to flavor the triangular biscuits by rubbing them with a little cheese or freeze-dried liver.

To teach come, call your dog, open your arms as a welcoming signal, wave a toy or a treat and praise for every step in your direction.

If stuffed chew toys are reserved especially for times the dog is confined, the puppydog will soon learn to enjoy quiet moments in her doggy den and she will quickly develop a chew-toy habit— a good habit! This is a simple *autoshaping* process; all the owner has to do is set up the situation and the dog all but trains herself— easy and effective. Even when the dog is given run of the house, her first inclination will be to indulge her rewarding chew-toy habit rather than destroy less-attractive household articles, such as curtains, carpets, chairs and compact disks. Similarly, a chew-toy chewer will be less inclined to scratch and chew herself excessively. Also, if the dog busies herself as a recreational chewer, she will be less inclined to develop into a recreational barker or digger when left at home alone.

Stuff a number of chew toys whenever the dog is left confined and remove the extra-special-tasting treats when you return. Your dog will now amuse herself with her chew toys before falling asleep and then resume playing with her chew toys when she expects you to return. Since most owner-absent misbehavior happens right after you leave and right before your expected return, your puppydog will now be conveniently preoccupied with her chew toys at these times.

Come and Sit

Most puppies will happily approach virtually anyone, whether called or not; that is, until they collide with adolescence and develop other more important doggy interests, such as sniffing a multiplicity of exquisite odors on the grass. Your mission, Mr./Ms. Owner, is to teach and reward the pup for coming reliably, willingly and happily when called—and you have just three months to get it done. Unless adequately reinforced, your puppy's tendency to approach people will self-destruct by adolescence.

Call your dog ("Tina, come!"), open your arms (and maybe squat down) as a welcoming signal, waggle a treat or toy as a lure and reward the puppydog when she comes running. Do not wait to praise the dog until she reaches you—she may come 95 percent of the way and then run off after some distraction. Instead, praise the dog's *first* step towards you and continue praising enthusiastically for *every* step she takes in your direction.

When the rapidly approaching puppy dog is three lengths away from impact, instruct her to sit ("Tina, sit!") and hold the lure in front of you in an outstretched hand to prevent her from hitting you mid-chest and knocking you flat on your back! As Tina decelerates to nose the lure, move the treat upwards and backwards just over her muzzle with an upwards motion of your extended arm (palm-upwards). As the dog looks up to follow the lure, she will sit down (if she jumps up, you are holding the lure too high). Praise the dog for sitting. Move backwards and call her again. Repeat this many times over, always praising when Tina comes and sits; on occasion, reward her.

For the first couple of trials, use a training treat both as a lure to entice the dog to come and sit and as a reward for doing so. Thereafter, try to use different items as lures and rewards. For example, lure the dog with a Kong or Frisbee but reward her with a food treat. Or lure the dog with a food treat but pat her and throw a tennis ball as a reward. After just a few repetitions, dispense with the lures and rewards; the dog will begin to respond willingly to your verbal requests and hand signals just for the prospect of praise from your heart and affection from your hands.

Instruct every family member, friend and visitor how to get the dog to come and sit. Invite people over for a series of pooch parties; do not keep the pup a secret— let other people enjoy this puppy, and let the pup enjoy other people. Puppydog parties are not only fun, they easily attract a lot of people to help *you* train *your* dog. Unless you teach your dog how to meet people, that is, to sit for greetings, no doubt the dog will resort to jumping up. Then you and the visitors will get annoyed, and the dog will be punished. This is not fair. *Send out those invitations for puppy parties and teach your dog to be mannerly and socially acceptable.*

Even though your dog quickly masters obedient recalls in the house, her reliability may falter when playing in the backyard or local park. Ironically, it is *the owner* who has unintentionally trained the dog *not* to respond in these instances. By allowing the dog to play and run around and otherwise have a good time, but then to call the dog to put her on leash to take her home, the dog quickly learns playing is fun but training is a drag. Thus, playing in the park becomes a severe distraction, which works against training. Bad news!

Instead, whether playing with the dog off leash or on leash, request her to come at frequent intervals—say, every minute or so. On most occasions, praise and pet the dog for a few seconds while she is sitting, then tell her to go play again. For especially fast recalls, offer a couple of training treats and take the time to praise and pet the dog enthusiastically before releasing her. The dog will learn that coming when called is not necessarily the end of the play session, and neither is it the end of the world; rather, it signals an enjoyable, quality time-out with the owner before resuming play once more. In fact, playing in the park now becomes a very effective life-reward, which works to facilitate training by reinforcing each obedient and timely recall. Good news!

Sit, Down, Stand and Rollover

Teaching the dog a variety of body positions is easy for owner and dog, impressive for spectators and extremely useful for all. Using lure-reward techniques, it is possible to train several positions at once to verbal commands or hand signals (which impress the socks off onlookers).

Sit and ***down***—the two control commands—prevent or resolve nearly a hundred behavior problems. For example, if the dog happily and obediently sits or lies down when requested, she cannot jump on visitors, dash out the front door, run around and chase her tail, pester other dogs, harass cats or annoy family, friends or strangers. Additionally, "Sit" or "Down" are the best emergency commands for off-leash control.

It is easier to teach and maintain a reliable sit than maintain a reliable recall. *Sit* is the purest and simplest of commands—either the dog is sitting or she is not. If there is any change of circumstances or potential danger in the park, for example, simply instruct the dog to sit. If she sits, you have a number of options: Allow the dog to resume playing when she is safe, walk up and put the dog on leash or call the dog. The dog will be much more likely to come when called if she has already acknowledged her compliance by sitting. If the dog does not sit in the park—train her to!

Stand and ***rollover-stay*** are the two positions for examining the dog. Your veterinarian will love you to distraction if you take a little time to teach the dog to stand still and roll over and play possum. Also, your vet bills will be smaller because it will take the veterinarian less time to examine your dog. The rollover-stay is an especially useful command and is really just a variation of the down-stay: Whereas the dog lies prone in the traditional down, she lies supine in the rollover-stay.

As with teaching come and sit, the training techniques to teach the dog to assume all other body positions on cue are user-friendly and dog-friendly. Simply give the appropriate request, lure the dog into the desired body position using a training treat or toy and then *praise* (and maybe reward) the dog as soon as she complies. Try not to touch the dog to get her to respond. If you teach the dog by guiding her into position, the dog will quickly learn that rump-pressure means sit, for example, but as yet you still have no control over your dog if she is just 6 feet away. It will still be necessary to teach the dog to sit on request. So do not make training a time-consuming two-step process; instead, teach the dog to sit to a verbal request or hand signal from the outset. Once the dog sits willingly when requested, by all means use your hands to pet the dog when she does so.

To teach **down** when the dog is already sitting, say "Tina, down!," hold the lure in one hand (palm down) and lower that hand to the floor between the dog's forepaws. As the dog lowers her head to follow the lure, slowly move the lure away from the dog just a fraction (in front of her paws). The dog will lie down as she stretches her nose forward to follow the lure. Praise the dog when she does so. If the dog stands up, you pulled the lure away too far and too quickly.

When teaching the dog to lie down from the standing position, say "Down" and lower the lure to the floor as before. Once the dog has lowered her forequarters and assumed a play bow, gently and slowly move the lure *towards* the dog between her forelegs. Praise the dog as soon as her rear end plops down.

After just a couple of trials it will be possible to alternate sits and downs and have the dog energetically perform doggy push-ups. Praise the dog a lot, and after half a dozen or so push-ups reward the dog with a training treat or toy. You will notice the more energetically you move your arm—upwards (palm up) to get the dog to sit, and downwards (palm down) to get the dog to lie down—the more energetically the dog responds to your requests. Now try training the dog in silence and you will notice she has also learned to respond to hand signals. Yeah! Not too shabby for the first session.

To teach **stand** from the sitting position, say "Tina, stand," slowly move the lure half a dog-length away from the dog's nose, keeping it at nose level, and praise the dog as she stands to follow the lure. As soon

115

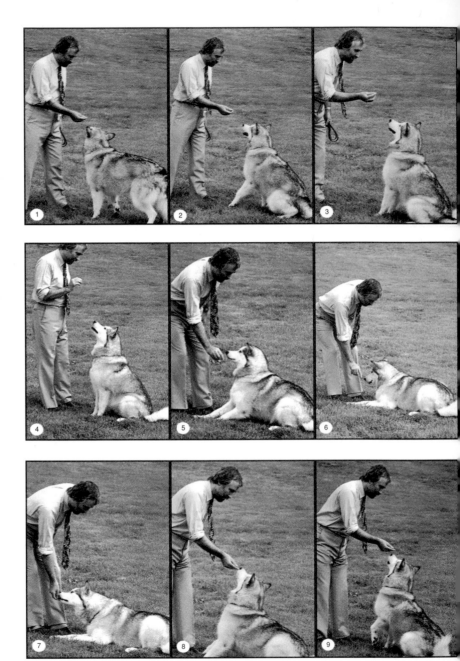

Using a food lure to teach sit, down and stand. 1) "Phoenix, sit." 2) Hand palm upwards, move lure up and back over dog's muzzle. 3) "Good sit, Phoenix!" 4) "Phoenix, down." 5) Hand palm downwards, move lure down to lie between dog's forepaws. 6) "Phoenix, off. Good down, Phoenix!" 7) "Phoenix, sit!" 8) Palm upwards, move lure up and back, keeping it close to dog's muzzle. 9) "Good sit, Phoenix!"

0) "Phoenix, stand!" 11) Move lure away from dog at nose height, then lower it a tad. 12) "Phoenix, ff! Good stand, Phoenix!" 13) "Phoenix, down!" 14) Hand palm downwards, move lure down to lie etween dog's forepaws. 15) "Phoenix, off! Good down-stay, Phoenix!" 16) "Phoenix, stand!" 17) Move are away from dog's muzzle up to nose height. 18) "Phoenix, off! Good stand-stay, Phoenix. Now we'll nake the vet and groomer happy!"

as the dog stands, lower the lure to just beneath the dog's chin to entice her to look down; otherwise she will stand and then sit immediately. To prompt the dog to stand from the down position, move the lure half a dog-length upwards and away from the dog, holding the lure at standing nose height from the floor.

Teaching *rollover* is best started from the down position, with the dog lying on one side, or at least with both hind legs stretched out on the same side. Say "Tina, bang!" and move the lure backwards and alongside the dog's muzzle to her elbow (on the side of her outstretched hind legs). Once the dog looks to the side and backwards, very slowly move the lure upwards to the dog's shoulder and backbone. Tickling the dog in the goolies (groin area) often invokes a reflex-raising of the hind leg as an appeasement gesture, which facilitates the tendency to roll over. If you move the lure too quickly and the dog jumps into the standing position, have patience and start again. As soon as the dog rolls onto her back, keep the lure stationary and mesmerize the dog with a relaxing tummy rub.

To teach *rollover-stay* when the dog is standing or moving, say "Tina, bang!" and give the appropriate hand signal (with index finger pointed and thumb cocked in true Sam Spade fashion), then in one fluid movement lure her to first lie down and then rollover-stay as above.

Teaching the dog to *stay* in each of the above four positions becomes a piece of cake after first teaching the dog not to worry at the toy or treat training lure. This is best accomplished by hand feeding dinner kibble. Hold a piece of kibble firmly in your hand and softly instruct "Off!" Ignore any licking and slobbering *for however long the dog worries at the treat,* but say "Take it!" and offer the kibble *the instant* the dog breaks contact with her muzzle. Repeat this a few times, and then up the ante and insist the dog remove her muzzle for one whole second before offering the kibble. Then progressively refine your criteria and have the dog not touch your hand (or treat) for longer and longer periods on each trial, such as for two seconds, four seconds, then six, ten, fifteen, twenty, thirty seconds and so on.

The dog soon learns: (1) worrying at the treat never gets results, whereas (2) noncontact is often rewarded after a variable time lapse.

Teaching *"Off!"* has many useful applications in its own right. Additionally, instructing the dog not to touch a training lure often produces spontaneous and magical stays. Request the dog to stand-stay, for example, and not to touch the lure. At first set your sights on a short two-second stay before rewarding the dog. (Remember, every long journey begins with a single step.) However, on subsequent trials, gradually and progressively increase the length of stay required to receive a reward. In no time at all your dog will stand calmly for a minute or so.

Relevancy Training

Once you have taught the dog what you expect her to do when requested to come, sit, lie down, stand, roll-over and stay, the time is right to teach the dog *why* she should comply with your wishes. The secret is to have many (*many*) extremely short training interludes (two to five seconds each) at numerous (*numerous*) times during the course of the dog's day. Especially work with the dog immediately *before* the dog's good times and *during* the dog's good times. For example, ask your dog to sit and/or lie down each time before opening doors, serving meals, offering treats and tummy rubs; ask the dog to perform a few controlled doggy push-ups before letting her off leash or throwing a tennis ball; and perhaps request the dog to sit-down-sit-stand-down-stand-rollover before inviting her to cuddle on the couch.

Similarly, request the dog to sit many times during play or on walks, and in no time at all the dog will be only too pleased to follow your instructions because she has learned that a compliant response heralds all sorts of goodies. Basically all you are trying to teach the dog is how to say please: "Please throw the tennis ball. Please may I snuggle on the couch."

Remember, it is important to keep training interludes short and to have many short sessions each and every day. The shortest (and most useful) session comprises asking the dog to sit and then go play during a play session. When trained this way, your dog will soon associate training with good times. In fact, the dog may be unable to distinguish between training and good times and, indeed, there should be no distinction. The warped concept that training involves forcing the dog to comply and/or dominating her will is totally at odds with the picture of a truly well-trained dog. In reality, enjoying a game of training with a dog is no different from enjoying a game of backgammon or tennis with a friend; and walking with a dog should be no different from strolling with a spouse, or with buddies on the golf course.

Walk by Your Side

Many people attempt to teach a dog to heel by putting her on a leash and physically correcting the dog when she makes mistakes. There are a number of things seriously wrong with this approach, the first being that most people do not want precision heeling; rather, they simply want the dog to follow or walk by their side. Second, when physically restrained during "training," even though the dog may grudgingly mope by your side when "handcuffed" on leash, let's see what happens when she is off leash. History! The dog is in the next county because she never enjoyed walking with you on leash and you have no control over her off leash. So let's just teach the dog off leash from the outset to *want* to walk with us. Third, if the dog has not been trained to heel, it is a trifle hasty to think about punishing the poor dog for making mistakes and breaking heeling rules she didn't even know existed. This is simply not fair! Surely, if the dog had been adequately taught how to heel, she would seldom make mistakes and hence there would be no need to correct the dog. Remember, each mistake and each correction (punishment) advertise the trainer's inadequacy, not the dog's. The dog is not stubborn, she is not stupid and she is not bad. Even if she were, she would still require training, so let's train her properly.

Let's teach the dog to *enjoy* following us and to *want* to walk by our side off leash. Then it will be easier to teach high-precision off-leash heeling patterns if desired. Before going on outdoor walks, it is necessary to teach the dog not to pull. Then it becomes easy to teach on-leash walking and heeling because the dog already wants to walk with you, she is familiar with the desired walking and heeling positions and she knows not to pull.

FOLLOWING

Start by training your dog to follow you. Many puppies will follow if you simply walk away from them and maybe click your fingers or chuckle. Adult dogs may require additional enticement to stimulate them to follow, such as a training lure or, at the very least, a lively trainer. To teach the dog to follow: (1) keep walking and (2) walk away from the dog. If the dog attempts to lead or lag, change pace; slow down if the dog forges too far ahead, but speed up if she lags too far behind. Say "Steady!" or "Easy!" each time before you slow down and "Quickly!" or "Hustle!" each time before you speed up, and the dog will learn to change pace on cue. If the dog lags or leads too far, or if she wanders right or left, simply walk quickly in the opposite direction and maybe even run away from the dog and hide.

Practicing is a lot of fun; you can set up a course in your home, yard or park to do this. Indoors, entice the dog to follow upstairs, into a bedroom, into the bathroom, downstairs, around the living room couch, zigzagging between dining room chairs and into the kitchen for dinner. Outdoors, get the dog to follow around park benches, trees, shrubs and along walkways and lines in the grass. (For safety outdoors, it is advisable to attach a long line on the dog, but never exert corrective tension on the line.)

Remember, following has a lot to do with attitude—
your attitude! Most probably your dog will *not* want to
follow Mr. Grumpy Troll with the personality of wilted
lettuce. Lighten up—walk with a jaunty step, whistle a
happy tune, sing, skip and tell jokes to your dog and
she will be right there by your side.

BY YOUR SIDE

It is smart to train the dog to walk close on one side or
the other—either side will do, your choice. When walking, jogging or cycling, it is generally bad news to have
the dog suddenly cut in front of you. In fact, I train my
dogs to walk "By my side" and "Other side"—both very
useful instructions. It is possible to position the dog
fairly accurately by looking to the appropriate side and
clicking your fingers or slapping your thigh on that
side. A precise positioning may be attained by holding
a training lure, such as a chew toy, tennis ball or food
treat. Stop and stand still several times throughout the
walk, just as you would when window shopping or
meeting a friend. Use the lure to make sure the dog
slows down and stays close whenever you stop.

When teaching the dog to heel, we generally want
her to sit in heel position when we stop. Teach heel

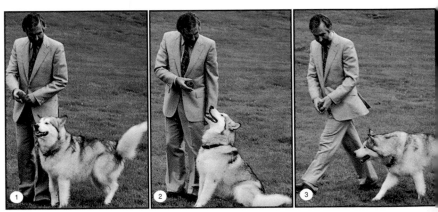

*Using a toy to teach sit-heel-sit sequences: 1) "Phoenix, sit!" Standing still, move lure up and back over dog's
muzzle . . . 2) to position dog sitting in heel position on your left side. 3) Say "Phoenix, heel!" and walk ahead,
wagging lure in left hand. Change lure to right hand in preparation for sit signal. Say "Sit" and then . . .*

position at the standstill and the dog will learn that the default heel position is sitting by your side (left or right—your choice, unless you wish to compete in obedience trials, in which case the dog must heel on the left).

Several times a day, stand up and call your dog to come and sit in heel position—"Tina, heel!" For example, instruct the dog to come to heel each time there are commercials on TV, or each time you turn a page of a novel, and the dog will get it in a single evening.

Practice straight-line heeling and turns separately. With the dog sitting at heel, teach her to turn in place. After each quarter-turn, half-turn or full turn in place, lure the dog to sit at heel. Now it's time for short straight-line heeling sequences, no more than a few steps at a time. Always think of heeling in terms of sit-heel-sit sequences—start and end with the dog in position and do your best to keep her there when moving. Progressively increase the number of steps in each sequence. When the dog remains close for 20 yards of straight-line heeling, it is time to add a few turns and then sign up for a happy-heeling obedience class to get some advice from the experts.

4) use hand signal to lure dog to sit as you stop. Eventually, dog will sit automatically at heel whenever you stop. 5) "Good dog!"

No Pulling on Leash

You can start teaching your dog not to pull on leash anywhere—in front of the television or outdoors—but regardless of location, you must not take a single step with tension in the leash. For a reason known only to dogs, even just a couple of paces of pulling on leash is intrinsically motivating and diabolically rewarding. Instead, attach the leash to the dog's collar, grasp the other end firmly with both hands held close to your chest, and stand still—do not budge an inch. Have somebody watch you with a stopwatch to time your progress, or else you will never believe this will work and so you will not even try the exercise, and your shoulder and the dog's neck will be traumatized for years to come.

Stand still and wait for the dog to stop pulling, and to sit and/or lie down. All dogs stop pulling and sit eventually. Most take only a couple of minutes; the all-time record is 22½ minutes. Time how long it takes. Gently praise the dog when she stops pulling, and as soon as she sits, enthusiastically praise the dog and take just one step forward, then immediately stand still. This single step usually demonstrates the ballistic reinforcing nature of pulling on leash; most dogs explode to the end of the leash, so be prepared for the strain. Stand firm and wait for the dog to sit again. Repeat this half a dozen times and you will probably notice a progressive reduction in the force of the dog's one-step explosions and a radical reduction in the time it takes for the dog to sit each time.

As the dog learns "Sit we go" and "Pull we stop," she will begin to walk forward calmly with each single step and automatically sit when you stop. Now try two steps before you stop. Wooooooo! Scary! When the dog has mastered two steps at a time, try for three. After each success, progressively increase the number of steps in the sequence: try four steps and then six, eight, ten and twenty steps before stopping. Congratulations! You are now walking the dog on leash.

Whenever walking with the dog (off leash or on leash), make sure you stop periodically to practice a few position commands and stays before instructing the dog to "Walk on!" (Remember, you want the dog to be compliant everywhere, not just in the kitchen when her dinner is at hand.) For example, stopping every 25 yards to briefly train the dog amounts to over 200 training interludes within a single 3-mile stroll. And each training session is in a different location. You will not believe the improvement within just the first mile of the first walk.

To put it another way, integrating training into a walk offers 200 separate opportunities to use the continuance of the walk as a reward to reinforce the dog's education. Moreover, some training interludes may comprise continuing education for the dog's walking skills: Alternate short periods of the dog walking calmly by your side with periods when the dog is allowed to sniff and investigate the environment. Now sniffing odors on the grass and meeting other dogs become rewards which reinforce the dog's calm and mannerly demeanor. Good Lord! Whatever next? Many enjoyable walks together of course. Happy trails!

THE IMPORTANCE OF TRICKS

Nothing will improve a dog's quality of life better than having a few tricks under her belt. Teaching any trick expands the dog's vocabulary, which facilitates communication and improves the owner's control. Also, specific tricks help prevent and resolve specific behavior problems. For example, by teaching the dog to fetch her toys, the dog learns carrying a toy makes the owner happy and, therefore, will be more likely to chew her toy than other inappropriate items.

More important, teaching tricks prompts owners to lighten up and train with a sunny disposition. Really, tricks should be no different from any other behaviors we put on cue. But they are. When teaching tricks, owners have a much sweeter attitude, which in turn motivates the dog and improves her willingness to comply. The dog feels tricks are a blast, but formal commands are a drag. In fact, tricks are so enjoyable, they may be used as rewards in training by asking the dog to come, sit and down-stay and then rollover for a tummy rub. Go on, try it: Crack a smile and even giggle when the dog promptly and willingly lies down and stays.

Most important, performing tricks prompts onlookers to smile and giggle. Many people are scared of dogs, especially large ones. And nothing can be more off-putting for a dog than to be constantly confronted by strangers who don't like her because of her size or the way she looks. Uneasy people put the dog on edge, causing her to back off and bark, only frightening people all the more. And so a vicious circle develops, with the people's fear fueling the dog's fear *and vice versa*. Instead, tie a pink ribbon to your dog's collar and practice all sorts of tricks on walks and in the park, and you will be pleasantly amazed how it changes people's attitudes toward your friendly dog. The dog's repertoire of tricks is limited only by the trainer's imagination. Below I have described three of my favorites:

SPEAK AND SHUSH

The training sequence involved in teaching a dog to bark on request is no different from that used when training any behavior on cue: request—lure—response—reward. As always, the secret of success lies in finding an effective lure. If the dog always barks at the doorbell, for example, say "Rover, speak!", have an accomplice ring the doorbell, then reward the dog for barking. After a few woofs, ask Rover to "Shush!", waggle a food treat under her nose (to entice her to sniff and thus to shush), praise her when quiet and eventually offer the treat as a reward. Alternate "Speak" and "Shush," progressively increasing the length of shush-time between each barking bout.

PLAY BOW

With the dog standing, say "Bow!" and lower the food lure (palm upwards) to rest between the dog's forepaws. Praise as the dog lowers her forequarters and sternum to the ground (as when teaching the down), but then lure the dog to stand and offer the treat. On successive trials, gradually increase the length of time the dog is required to remain in the play bow posture in order to gain a food reward. If the dog's rear end collapses into a down, say nothing and offer no reward; simply start over.

BE A BEAR

With the dog sitting backed into a corner to prevent her from toppling over backwards, say "Be a bear!" With bent paw and palm down, raise a lure upwards and backwards along the top of the dog's muzzle. Praise the dog when she sits up on her haunches and offer the treat as a reward. To prevent the dog from standing on her hind legs, keep the lure closer to the dog's muzzle. On each trial, progressively increase the length of time the dog is required to sit up to receive a food reward. Since lure-reward training is so easy, teach the dog to stand and walk on her hind legs as well!

Teaching "Be a Bear"

chapter 9

Getting
Active
with your Dog

by Bardi McLennan

Once you and your dog have graduated from basic obedience training and are beginning to work together as a team, you can take part in the growing world of dog activities. There are so many fun things to do with your dog! Just remember, people and dogs don't always learn at the same pace, so don't be upset if you (or your dog) need more than two basic training courses before your team becomes operational. Even smart dogs don't go straight to college from kindergarten!

Just as there are events geared to certain types of dogs, so there are ones that are more appealing to certain types of people. In some

128

activities, you give the commands and your dog does the work (upland game hunting is one example), while in others, such as agility, you'll both get a workout. You may want to aim for prestigious titles to add to your dog's name, or you may want nothing more than the sheer enjoyment of being around other people and their dogs. Passive or active, participation has its own rewards.

Consider your dog's physical capabilities when looking into any of the canine activities. It's easy to see that a Basset Hound is not built for the racetrack, nor would a Chihuahua be the breed of choice for pulling a sled. A loyal dog will attempt almost anything you ask him to do, so it is up to you to know your dog's limitations. A dog must be physically sound in order to compete at any level in athletic activities, and being mentally sound is a definite plus. Advanced age, however, may not be a deterrent. Many dogs still hunt and herd at ten or twelve years of age. It's entirely possible for dogs to be "fit at 50." Take your dog for a checkup, explain to your vet the type of activity you have in mind and be guided by his or her findings.

All dogs seem to love playing flyball.

You needn't be restricted to breed-specific sports if it's only fun you're after. Certain AKC activities are limited to designated breeds; however, as each new trial, test or sport has grown in popularity, so has the variety of breeds encouraged to participate at a fun level.

But don't shortchange your fun, or that of your dog, by thinking only of the basic function of her breed. Once a dog has learned how to learn, she can be taught to do just about anything as long as the size of the dog is right for the job and you both think it is fun and rewarding. In other words, you are a team.

To get involved in any of the activities detailed in this chapter, look for the names and addresses of the organizations that sponsor them in Chapter 13. You can also ask your breeder or a local dog trainer for contacts.

You can compete in obedience trials with a well trained dog.

Official American Kennel Club Activities

The following tests and trials are some of the events sanctioned by the AKC and sponsored by various dog clubs. Your dog's expertise will be rewarded with impressive titles. You can participate just for fun, or be competitive and go for those awards.

OBEDIENCE

Training classes begin with pups as young as three months of age in kindergarten puppy training, then advance to pre-novice (all exercises on lead) and go on to novice, which is where you'll start off-lead work. In obedience classes dogs learn to sit, stay, heel and come through a variety of exercises. Once you've got the basics down, you can enter obedience trials and work toward earning your dog's first degree, a C.D. (Companion Dog).

The next level is called "Open," in which jumps and retrieves perk up the dog's interest. Passing grades in competition at this level earn a C.D.X. (Companion Dog Excellent). Beyond that lies the goal of the most ambitious—Utility (U.D. and even U.D.X. or OTCh, an Obedience Champion).

AGILITY

All dogs can participate in the latest canine sport to have gained worldwide popularity for its fun and excitement, agility. It began in England as a canine version of horse show-jumping, but because dogs are more agile and able to perform on verbal commands, extra feats were added such as climbing, balancing and racing through tunnels or in and out of weave poles. Many of the obstacles (regulation or homemade) can be set up in your own backyard. If the agility bug bites, you could end up in international competition!

For starters, your dog should be obedience trained, even though, in the beginning, the lessons may all be taught on lead. Once the dog understands the commands (and you do, too), it's as easy as guiding the dog over a prescribed course, one obstacle at a time. In competition, the race is against the clock, so wear your running shoes! The dog starts with 200 points and the judge deducts for infractions and misadventures along the way.

All dogs seem to love agility and respond to it as if they were being turned loose in a playground paradise. Your dog's enthusiasm will be contagious; agility turns into great fun for dog and owner.

FIELD TRIALS AND HUNTING TESTS

There are field trials and hunting tests for the sporting breeds—retrievers, spaniels and pointing breeds, and for some hounds—Bassets, Beagles and Dachshunds. Field trials are competitive events that test a dog's ability to perform the functions for which she was bred. Hunting tests, which are open to retrievers,

---

TITLES AWARDED BY THE AKC

Conformation: Ch. (Champion)

Obedience: CD (Companion Dog); CDX (Companion Dog Excellent); UD (Utility Dog); UDX (Utility Dog Excellent); OTCh. (Obedience Trial Champion)

Field: JH (Junior Hunter); SH (Senior Hunter); MH (Master Hunter); AFCh. (Amateur Field Champion); FCh. (Field Champion)

Lure Coursing: JC (Junior Courser); SC (Senior Courser)

Herding: HT (Herding Tested); PT (Pre-Trial Tested); HS (Herding Started); HI (Herding Intermediate); HX (Herding Excellent); HCh. (Herding Champion)

Tracking: TD (Tracking Dog); TDX (Tracking Dog Excellent)

Agility: NAD (Novice Agility); OAD (Open Agility); ADX (Agility Excellent); MAX (Master Agility)

Earthdog Tests: JE (Junior Earthdog); SE (Senior Earthdog); ME (Master Earthdog)

Canine Good Citizen: CGC

Combination: DC (Dual Champion—Ch. and Fch.); TC (Triple Champion—Ch., Fch., and OTCh.)

spaniels and pointing breeds only, are noncompetitive and are a means of judging the dog's ability as well as that of the handler.

Hunting is a very large and complex part of canine sports, and if you own one of the breeds that hunts, the events are a great treat for your dog and you. He gets to do what he was bred for, and you get to work with him and watch him do it. You'll be proud of and amazed at what your dog can do.

Fortunately, the AKC publishes a series of booklets on these events, which outline the rules and regulations and include a glossary of the sometimes complicated terms. The AKC also publishes newsletters for field trialers and hunting test enthusiasts. The United Kennel Club (UKC) also has informative materials for the hunter and his dog.

Retrievers and other sporting breeds get to do what they're bred to in hunting tests.

HERDING TESTS AND TRIALS

Herding, like hunting, dates back to the first known uses man made of dogs. The interest in herding today is widespread, and if you own a herding breed, you can join in the activity. Herding dogs are tested for their natural skills to keep a flock of ducks, sheep or cattle together. If your dog shows potential, you can start at the testing level, where your dog can earn a title for showing an inherent herding ability. With training you can advance to the trial level, where your dog should be capable of controlling even difficult livestock in diverse situations.

LURE COURSING

The AKC Tests and Trials for Lure Coursing are open to traditional sighthounds—Greyhounds, Whippets,

Borzoi, Salukis, Afghan Hounds, Ibizan Hounds and Scottish Deerhounds—as well as to Basenjis and Rhodesian Ridgebacks. Hounds are judged on overall ability, follow, speed, agility and endurance. This is possibly the most exciting of the trials for spectators, because the speed and agility of the dogs is awesome to watch as they chase the lure (or "course") in heats of two or three dogs at a time.

TRACKING

Tracking is another activity in which almost any dog can compete because every dog that sniffs the ground when taken outdoors is, in fact, tracking. The hard part comes when the rules as to what, when and where the dog tracks are determined by a person, not the dog! Tracking tests cover a large area of fields, woods and roads. The tracks are laid hours before the dogs go to work on them, and include "tricks" like cross-tracks and sharp turns. If you're interested in search-and-rescue work, this is the place to start.

This tracking dog is hot on the trail.

EARTHDOG TESTS FOR SMALL TERRIERS AND DACHSHUNDS

These tests are open to Australian, Bedlington, Border, Cairn, Dandie Dinmont, Smooth and Wire Fox, Lakeland, Norfolk, Norwich, Scottish, Sealyham, Skye, Welsh and West Highland White Terriers as well as Dachshunds. The dogs need no prior training for this terrier sport. There is a qualifying test on the day of the event, so dog and handler learn the rules on the spot. These tests, or "digs," sometimes end with informal races in the late afternoon.

Here are some of the extracurricular obedience and
racing activities that are not regulated by the AKC or
UKC, but are generally run by clubs or a group of dog
fanciers and are often open to all.

Canine Freestyle This activity is something new on
the scene and is variously likened to dancing, dressage
or ice skating. It is meant to show the athleticism of the
dog, but also requires showmanship on the part of the
dog's handler. If you and your dog like to ham it up for
friends, you might want to look into freestyle.

*Lure coursing
lets sighthounds
do what they do
best—run!*

Scent Hurdle Racing Scent hurdle racing is purely a
fun activity sponsored by obedience clubs with members forming competing teams. The height of the hurdles is based on the size of the shortest dog on the
team. On a signal, one team dog is released on each of
two side-by-side courses and must clear every hurdle
before picking up its own dumbbell from a platform
and returning over the jumps to the handler. As each
dog returns, the next on that team is sent. Of course,
that is what the dogs are supposed to do. When the
dogs improvise (going under or around the hurdles,
stealing another dog's dumbbell, and so forth), it no
doubt frustrates the handlers, but just adds to the fun
for everyone else.

Flyball This type of racing is similar, but after negoti-
ating the four hurdles, the dog comes to a flyball box,
steps on a lever that releases a tennis ball into the air,

catches the ball and returns over the hurdles to the starting point. This game also becomes extremely fun for spectators because the dogs sometimes cheat by catching a ball released by the dog in the next lane. Three titles can be earned—Flyball Dog (F.D.), Flyball Dog Excellent (F.D.X.) and Flyball Dog Champion (Fb.D.Ch.)—all awarded by the North American Flyball Association, Inc.

Dogsledding The name conjures up the Rocky Mountains or the frigid North, but you can find dogsled clubs in such unlikely spots as Maryland, North Carolina and Virginia! Dogsledding is primarily for the Nordic breeds such as the Alaskan Malamutes, Siberian Huskies and Samoyeds, but other breeds can try. There are some practical backyard applications to this sport, too. With parental supervision, almost any strong dog could pull a child's sled.

Coming over the A-frame on an agility course.

These are just some of the many recreational ways you can get to know and understand your multifaceted dog better and have fun doing it.

chapter 10

Your Dog
and your
Family

by Bardi McLennan

Adding a dog automatically increases your family by one, no matter whether you live alone in an apartment or are part of a mother, father and six kids household. The single-person family is fair game for numerous and varied canine misconceptions as to who is dog and who pays the bills, whereas a dog in a houseful of children will consider himself to be just one of the gang, littermates all. One dog and one child may give a dog reason to believe they are both kids or both dogs.

Either interpretation requires parental supervision and sometimes speedy intervention.

As soon as one paw goes through the door into your home, Rufus (or Rufina) has to make many adjustments to become a part of your family. Your job is to make him fit in as painlessly as possible. An older dog may have some frame of reference from past experience, but to a 10-week-old puppy, everything is brand new: people, furniture, stairs, when and where people eat, sleep or watch TV, his own place and everyone else's space, smells, sounds, outdoors—everything!

Puppies, and newly acquired dogs of any age, do not need what we think of as "freedom." If you leave a new dog or puppy loose in the house, you will almost certainly return to chaotic destruction and the dog will forever after equate your homecoming with a time of punishment to be dreaded. It is unfair to give your dog what amounts to "freedom to get into trouble." Instead, confine him to a crate for brief periods of your absence (up to

three or four hours) and, for the long haul, a workday for example, confine him to one untrashable area with his own toys, a bowl of water and a radio left on (low) in another room.

Lots of pets get along with each other just fine.

For the first few days, when not confined, put Rufus on a long leash tied to your wrist or waist. This umbilical cord method enables the dog to learn all about you from your body language and voice, and to learn by his own actions which things in the house are NO! and which ones are rewarded by "Good dog." House-training will be easier with the pup always by your side. Speaking of which, accidents do happen. That goal of "completely housetrained" takes up to a year, or the length of time it takes the pup to mature.

The All-Adult Family

Most dogs in an adults-only household today are likely to be latchkey pets, with no one home all day but the dog. When you return after a tough day on the job, the dog can and should be your relaxation therapy. But going home can instead be a daily frustration.

Separation anxiety is a very common problem for the dog in a working household. It may begin with whines and barks of loneliness, but it will soon escalate into a frenzied destruction derby. That is why it is so important to set aside the time to teach a dog to relax when left alone in his confined area and to understand that he can trust you to return.

Let the dog get used to your work schedule in easy stages. Confine him to one room and go in and out of that room over and over again. Be casual about it. No physical, voice or eye contact. When the pup no longer even notices your comings and goings, leave the house for varying lengths of time, returning to stay home for a few minutes and gradually increasing the time away. This training can take days, but the dog is learning that you haven't left him forever and that he can trust you.

Any time you leave the dog, but especially during this training period, be casual about your departure. No anxiety-building fond farewells. Just "Bye" and go! Remember the "Good dog" when you return to find everything more or less as you left it.

If things are a mess (or even a disaster) when you return, greet the dog, take him outside to eliminate, and then put him in his crate while you clean up. Rant and rave in the shower! *Do not* punish the dog. You were not there when it happened, and the rule is: Only punish as you catch the dog in the act of wrongdoing. Obviously, it makes sense to get your latchkey puppy when you'll have a week or two to spend on these training essentials.

Family weekend activities should include Rufus whenever possible. Depending on the pup's age, now is the time for a long walk in the park, playtime in the backyard, a hike in the woods. Socializing is as important as health care, good food and physical exercise, so visiting Aunt Emma or Uncle Harry and the next-door neighbor's dog or cat is essential to developing an outgoing, friendly temperament in your pet.

If you are a single adult, socializing Rufus at home and away will prevent him from becoming overly protective of you (or just overly attached) and will also prevent such behavioral problems as dominance or fear of strangers.

Babies

Whether already here or on the way, babies figure larger than life in the eyes of a dog. If the dog is there first, let him in on all your baby preparations in the house. When baby arrives, let Rufus sniff any item of clothing that has been on the baby before Junior comes home. Then let Mom greet the dog first before introducing the new family member. Hold the baby down for the dog to see and sniff, but make sure someone's holding the dog on lead in case of any sudden moves. Don't play keep-away or tease the dog with the baby, which only invites undesirable jumping up.

The dog and the baby are "family," and for starters can be treated almost as equals. Things rapidly change, however, especially when baby takes to creeping around on all fours on the dog's turf or, better yet, has yummy pudding all over her face and hands! That's when a lot of things in the dog's and baby's lives become more separate than equal.

Dogs are perfect confidants.

Toddlers make terrible dog owners, but if you can't avoid the combination, use patient discipline (that is, positive teaching rather than punishment), and use time-outs before you run out of patience.

A dog and a baby (or toddler, or an assertive young child) should never be left alone together. Take the dog with you or confine him. With a baby or youngsters in the house, you'll have plenty of use for that wonderful canine safety device called a crate!

Young Children

Any dog in a house with kids will behave pretty much as the kids do, good or bad. But even good dogs and good children can get into trouble when play becomes rowdy and active.

Teach children how to play nicely with a puppy.

Legs bobbing up and down, shrill voices screeching, a ball hurtling overhead, all add up to exuberant frustration for a dog who's just trying to be part of the gang. In a pack of puppies, any legs or toys being chased would be caught by a set of teeth, and all the pups involved would understand that is how the game is played. Kids do not understand this, nor do parents tolerate it. Bring Rufus indoors before you have reason to regret it. This is time-out, not a punishment.

You can explain the situation to the children and tell them they must play quieter games until the puppy learns not to grab them with his mouth. Unfortunately, you can't explain it that easily to the dog. With adult supervision, they will learn how to play together.

Young children love to tease. Sticking their faces or wiggling their hands or fingers in the dog's face is teasing. To another person it might be just annoying, but it is threatening to a dog. There's another difference: We can make the child stop by an explanation, but the only way a dog can stop it is with a warning growl and then with teeth. Teasing is the major cause of children being bitten by their pets. Treat it seriously.

Older Children

The best age for a child to get a first dog is between the ages of 8 and 12. That's when kids are able to accept some real responsibility for their pet. Even so, take the child's vow of "I will never *ever* forget to feed (brush, walk, etc.) the dog" for what it's worth: a child's good intention at that moment. Most kids today have extra lessons, soccer practice, Little League, ballet, and so forth piled on top of school schedules. There will be many times when Mom will have to come to the dog's rescue. "I walked the dog for you so you can set the table for me" is one way to get around a missed appointment without laying on blame or guilt.

Kids in this age group make excellent obedience trainers because they are into the teaching/learning process themselves and they lack the self-consciousness of adults. Attending a dog show is something the whole family can enjoy, and watching Junior Showmanship may catch the eye of the kids. Older children can begin to get involved in many of the recreational activities that were reviewed in the previous chapter. Some of the agility obstacles, for example, can be set up in the backyard as a family project (with an adult making sure all the equipment is safe and secure for the dog).

Older kids are also beginning to look to the future, and may envision themselves as veterinarians or trainers or show dog handlers or writers of the next Lassie best-seller. Dogs are perfect confidants for these dreams. They won't tell a soul.

Other Pets

Introduce all pets tactfully. In a dog/cat situation, hold the dog, not the cat. Let two dogs meet on neutral turf—a stroll in the park or a walk down the street— with both on loose leads to permit all the normal canine ways of saying hello, including routine sniffing, circling, more sniffing, and so on. Small creatures such as hamsters, chinchillas or mice must be kept safe from their natural predators (dogs and cats).

Festive Family Occasions

Parties are great for people, but not necessarily for puppies. Until all the guests have arrived, put the dog in his crate or in a room where he won't be disturbed. A socialized dog can join the fun later as long as he's not underfoot, annoying guests or into the hors d'oeuvres.

There are a few dangers to consider, too. Doors opening and closing can allow a puppy to slip out unnoticed in the confusion, and you'll be organizing a search party instead of playing host or hostess. Party food and buffet service are not for dogs. Let Rufus party in his crate with a nice big dog biscuit.

At Christmas time, not only are tree decorations dangerous and breakable (and perhaps family heirlooms), but extreme caution should be taken with the lights, cords and outlets for the tree lights and any other festive lighting. Occasionally a dog lifts a leg, ignoring the fact that the tree is indoors. To avoid this, use a canine repellent, made for gardens, on the tree. Or keep him out of the tree room unless supervised. And whatever you do, *don't* invite trouble by hanging his toys on the tree!

Car Travel

Before you plan a vacation by car or RV with Rufus, be sure he enjoys car travel. Nothing spoils a holiday quicker than a carsick dog! Work within the dog's comfort level. Get in the car with the dog in his crate or attached to a canine car safety belt and just sit there until he relaxes. That's all. Next time, get in the car, turn on the engine and go nowhere. Just sit. When that is okay, turn on the engine and go around the block. Now you can go for a ride and include a stop where you get out, leaving the dog for a minute or two.

On a warm day, always park in the shade and leave windows open several inches. And return quickly. It only takes 10 minutes for a car to become an overheated steel death trap.

Motel or Pet Motel?

Not all motels or hotels accept pets, but you have a much better choice today than even a few years ago. To find a dog-friendly lodging, look at *On the Road Again With Man's Best Friend*, a series of directories that detail bed and breakfasts, inns, family resorts and other hotels/motels. Some places require a refundable deposit to cover any damage incurred by the dog. More B&Bs accept pets now, but some restrict the size.

If taking Rufus with you is not feasible, check out boarding kennels in your area. Your veterinarian may offer this service, or recommend a kennel or two he or she is familiar with. Go see the facilities for yourself, ask about exercise, diet, housing, and so on. Or, if you'd rather have Rufus stay home, look into bonded petsitters, many of whom will also bring in the mail and water your plants.

chapter 11

Your Dog
and your
Community

by Bardi McLennan

Step outside your home with your dog and you are no longer just family, you are both part of your community. This is when the phrase "responsible pet ownership" takes on serious implications. For starters, it means you pick up after your dog—not just occasionally, but every time your dog eliminates away from home. That means you have joined the Plastic Baggy Brigade! You always have plastic sandwich bags in your pocket and several in the car. It means you teach your kids how to use them, too. If you think this is "yucky," just imagine what the person (a non-doggy person) who inadvertently steps in the mess thinks!

Your responsibility extends to your neighbors: To their ears (no annoying barking); to their property (their garbage, their lawn, their flower beds, their cat—especially their cat); to their kids (on bikes, at play); to their kids' toys and sports equipment.

There are numerous dog-related laws, ranging from simple dog licensing and leash laws to those holding you liable for any physical injury or property damage done by your dog. These laws are in place to protect everyone in the community, including you and your dog. There are town ordinances and state laws which are by no means the same in all towns or all states. Ignorance of the law won't get you off the hook. The time to find out what the laws are where you live is now.

Be sure your dog's license is current. This is not just a good local ordinance, it can make the difference between finding your lost dog or not. Many states now require proof of rabies vaccination and that the dog has been spayed or neutered before issuing a license. At the same time, keep up the dog's annual immunizations.

Dressing your dog up makes him appealing to strangers.

Never let your dog run loose in the neighborhood. This will not only keep you on the right side of the leash law, it's the outdoor version of the rule about not giving your dog "freedom to get into trouble."

Good Canine Citizen

Sometimes it's hard for a dog's owner to assess whether or not the dog is sufficiently socialized to be accepted by the community at large. Does Rufus or Rufina display good, controlled behavior in public? The AKC's Canine Good Citizen program is available through many dog organizations. If your dog passes the test, the title "CGC" is earned.

The overall purpose is to turn your dog into a good neighbor and to teach you about your responsibility to your community as a dog owner. Here are the ten things your dog must do willingly:

1. Accept a stranger stopping to chat with you.
2. Sit and be petted by a stranger.
3. Allow a stranger to handle him or her as a groomer or veterinarian would.
4. Walk nicely on a loose lead.
5. Walk calmly through a crowd.
6. Sit and down on command, then stay in a sit or down position while you walk away.
7. Come when called.
8. Casually greet another dog.
9. React confidently to distractions.
10. Accept being left alone with someone other than you and not become overly agitated or nervous.

Schools and Dogs

Schools are getting involved with pet ownership on an educational level. It has been proven that children who are kind to animals are humane in their attitude toward other people as adults.

A dog is a child's best friend, and so children are often primary pet owners, if not the primary caregivers. Unfortunately, they are also the ones most often bitten by dogs. This occurs due to a lack of understanding that pets, no matter how sweet, cuddly and loving, are still animals. Schools, along with parents, dog clubs, dog fanciers and the AKC, are working to change all that with video programs for children not only in grade school, but in the nursery school and pre-kindergarten age group. Teaching youngsters how to be responsible dog owners is important community work. When your dog has a CGC, volunteer to take part in an educational classroom event put on by your dog club.

Boy Scout Merit Badge

A Merit Badge for Dog Care can be earned by any Boy Scout ages 11 to 18. The requirements are not easy, but amount to a complete course in responsible dog care and general ownership. Here are just a few of the things a Scout must do to earn that badge:

> Point out ten parts of the dog using the correct names.

> Give a report (signed by parent or guardian) on your care of the dog (feeding, food used, housing, exercising, grooming and bathing), plus what has been done to keep the dog healthy.

> Explain the right way to obedience train a dog, and demonstrate three comments.

> Several of the requirements have to do with health care, including first aid, handling a hurt dog, and the dangers of home treatment for a serious ailment.

> The final requirement is to know the local laws and ordinances involving dogs.

There are similar programs for Girl Scouts and 4-H members.

Local Clubs

Local dog clubs are no longer in existence just to put on a yearly dog show. Today, they are apt to be the hub of the community's involvement with pets. Dog clubs conduct educational forums with big-name speakers, stage demonstrations of canine talent in a busy mall and take dogs of various breeds to schools for classroom discussion.

The quickest way to feel accepted as a member in a club is to volunteer your services! Offer to help with something—anything—and watch your popularity (and your interest) grow.

Therapy Dogs

Once your dog has earned that essential CGC and reliably demonstrates a steady, calm temperament, you could look into what therapy dogs are doing in your area.

Therapy dogs go with their owners to visit patients at hospitals or nursing homes, generally remaining on leash but able to coax a pat from a stiffened hand, a smile from a blank face, a few words from sealed lips or a hug from someone in need of love.

Nursing homes cover a wide range of patient care. Some specialize in care of the elderly, some in the treatment of specific illnesses, some in physical therapy. Children's facilities also welcome visits from

Your dog can make a difference in lots of lives.

trained therapy dogs for boosting morale in their pediatric patients. Hospice care for the terminally ill and the at-home care of AIDS patients are other areas where this canine visiting is desperately needed. Therapy dog training comes first.

There is a lot more involved than just taking your nice friendly pooch to someone's bedside. Doing therapy dog work involves your own emotional stability as well as that of your dog. But once you have met all the requirements for this work, making the rounds once a week or once a month with your therapy dog is possibly the most rewarding of all community activities.

Disaster Aid

This community service is definitely not for everyone, partly because it is time-consuming. The initial training is rigorous, and there can be no let-up in the continuing workouts, because members are on call 24 hours a day to go wherever they are needed at a moment's notice. But if you think you would like to be able to assist in a disaster, look into search-and-rescue work. The network of search-and-rescue volunteers is worldwide, and all members of the American Rescue Dog Association (ARDA) who are qualified to do this work are volunteers who train and maintain their own dogs.

Physical Aid

Most people are familiar with Seeing Eye dogs, which serve as blind people's eyes, but not with all the other work that dogs are trained to do to assist the disabled. Dogs are also specially trained to pull wheelchairs, carry school books, pick up dropped objects, open and close doors. Some also are ears for the deaf. All these assistance-trained dogs, by the way, are allowed anywhere "No Pet" signs exist (as are therapy dogs when

Making the rounds with your therapy dog can be very rewarding.

properly identified). Getting started in any of this fascinating work requires a background in dog training and canine behavior, but there are also volunteer jobs ranging from answering the phone to cleaning out kennels to providing a foster home for a puppy. You have only to ask.

part four

Beyond
the
Basics

chapter 12

Recommended Reading

Books

ABOUT HEALTH CARE

Ackerman, Lowell. *Guide to Skin and Haircoat Problems in Dogs*. Loveland, Colo.: Alpine Publications, 1994.

Alderton, David. *The Dog Care Manual*. Hauppauge, N.Y.: Barron's Educational Series, Inc., 1986.

American Kennel Club. *American Kennel Club Dog Care and Training*. New York: Howell Book House, 1991.

Bamberger, Michelle, DVM. *Help! The Quick Guide to First Aid for Your Dog*. New York: Howell Book House, 1995.

Carlson, Delbert, DVM, and James Giffin, MD. *Dog Owner's Home Veterinary Handbook*. New York: Howell Book House, 1992.

DeBitetto, James, DVM, and Sarah Hodgson. *You & Your Puppy*. New York: Howell Book House, 1995.

Humphries, Jim, DVM. *Dr. Jim's Animal Clinic for Dogs*. New York: Howell Book House, 1994.

McGinnis, Terri. *The Well Dog Book*. New York: Random House, 1991.

Pitcairn, Richard and Susan. *Natural Health for Dogs*. Emmaus, Pa.: Rodale Press, 1982.

ABOUT DOG SHOWS

Hall, Lynn. *Dog Showing for Beginners*. New York: Howell Book House, 1994.

Nichols, Virginia Tuck. *How to Show Your Own Dog*. Neptune, N. J.: TFH, 1970.

Vanacore, Connie. *Dog Showing, An Owner's Guide*. New York: Howell Book House, 1990.

ABOUT TRAINING

Ammen, Amy. *Training in No Time.* New York: Howell Book House, 1995.

Baer, Ted. *Communicating With Your Dog.* Hauppauge, N.Y.: Barron's Educational Series, Inc., 1989.

Benjamin, Carol Lea. *Dog Problems.* New York: Howell Book House, 1989.

Benjamin, Carol Lea. *Dog Training for Kids.* New York: Howell Book House, 1988.

Benjamin, Carol Lea. *Mother Knows Best.* New York: Howell Book House, 1985.

Benjamin, Carol Lea. *Surviving Your Dog's Adolescence.* New York: Howell Book House, 1993.

Bohnenkamp, Gwen. *Manners for the Modern Dog.* San Francisco: Perfect Paws, 1990.

Dibra, Bashkim. *Dog Training by Bash.* New York: Dell, 1992.

Dunbar, Ian, PhD, MRCVS. *Dr. Dunbar's Good Little Dog Book,* James & Kenneth Publishers, 2140 Shattuck Ave. #2406, Berkeley, Calif. 94704. (510) 658–8588. Order from the publisher.

Dunbar, Ian, PhD, MRCVS. *How to Teach a New Dog Old Tricks,* James & Kenneth Publishers. Order from the publisher; address above.

Dunbar, Ian, PhD, MRCVS, and Gwen Bohnenkamp. Booklets on *Preventing Aggression; Housetraining; Chewing; Digging; Barking; Socialization; Fearfulness; and Fighting,* James & Kenneth Publishers. Order from the publisher; address above.

Evans, Job Michael. *People, Pooches and Problems.* New York: Howell Book House, 1991.

Kilcommons, Brian and Sarah Wilson. *Good Owners, Great Dogs.* New York: Warner Books, 1992.

McMains, Joel M. *Dog Logic—Companion Obedience.* New York: Howell Book House, 1992.

Rutherford, Clarice and David H. Neil, MRCVS. *How to Raise a Puppy You Can Live With.* Loveland, Colo.: Alpine Publications, 1982.

Volhard, Jack and Melissa Bartlett. *What All Good Dogs Should Know: The Sensible Way to Train.* New York: Howell Book House, 1991.

ABOUT BREEDING

Harris, Beth J. Finder. *Breeding a Litter, The Complete Book of Prenatal and Postnatal Care.* New York: Howell Book House, 1983.

Holst, Phyllis, DVM. *Canine Reproduction.* Loveland, Colo.: Alpine Publications, 1985.

Walkowicz, Chris and Bonnie Wilcox, DVM. *Successful Dog Breeding, The Complete Handbook of Canine Midwifery.* New York: Howell Book House, 1994.

ABOUT ACTIVITIES

American Rescue Dog Association. *Search and Rescue Dogs.* New York: Howell Book House, 1991.

Barwig, Susan and Stewart Hilliard. *Schutzhund.* New York: Howell Book House, 1991.

Beaman, Arthur S. *Lure Coursing.* New York: Howell Book House, 1994.

Daniels, Julie. *Enjoying Dog Agility—From Backyard to Competition.* New York: Doral Publishing, 1990.

Davis, Kathy Diamond. *Therapy Dogs.* New York: Howell Book House, 1992.

Gallup, Davis Anne. *Running With Man's Best Friend.* Loveland, Colo.: Alpine Publications, 1986.

Habgood, Dawn and Robert. *On the Road Again With Man's Best Friend.* New England, Mid-Atlantic, West Coast and Southeast editions. Selective guides to area bed and breakfasts, inns, hotels and resorts that welcome guests and their dogs. New York: Howell Book House, 1995.

Holland, Vergil S. *Herding Dogs.* New York: Howell Book House, 1994.

LaBelle, Charlene G. *Backpacking With Your Dog.* Loveland, Colo.: Alpine Publications, 1993.

Simmons-Moake, Jane. *Agility Training, The Fun Sport for All Dogs.* New York: Howell Book House, 1991.

Spencer, James B. *Hup! Training Flushing Spaniels the American Way.* New York: Howell Book House, 1992.

Spencer, James B. *Point! Training the All-Seasons Birddog.* New York: Howell Book House, 1995.

Tarrant, Bill. *Training the Hunting Retriever.* New York: Howell Book House, 1991.

Volhard, Jack and Wendy. *The Canine Good Citizen.* New York: Howell Book House, 1994.

General Titles

Haggerty, Captain Arthur J. *How to Get Your Pet Into Show Business.* New York: Howell Book House, 1994.

McLennan, Bardi. *Dogs and Kids, Parenting Tips.* New York: Howell Book House, 1993.

Moran, Patti J. *Pet Sitting for Profit, A Complete Manual for Professional Success.* New York: Howell Book House, 1992.

Scalisi, Danny and Libby Moses. *When Rover Just Won't Do, Over 2,000 Suggestions for Naming Your Dog*. New York: Howell Book House, 1993.

Sife, Wallace, PhD. *The Loss of a Pet*. New York: Howell Book House, 1993.

Wrede, Barbara J. *Civilizing Your Puppy*. Hauppauge, N.Y.: Barron's Educational Series, 1992.

Magazines

The AKC GAZETTE, The Official Journal for the Sport of Purebred Dogs. American Kennel Club, 51 Madison Ave., New York, NY.

Bloodlines Journal. United Kennel Club, 100 E. Kilgore Rd., Kalamazoo, MI.

Dog Fancy. Fancy Publications, 3 Burroughs, Irvine, CA 92718

Dog World. Maclean Hunter Publishing Corp., 29 N. Wacker Dr., Chicago, IL 60606.

Videos

"SIRIUS Puppy Training," by Ian Dunbar, PhD, MRCVS. James & Kenneth Publishers, 2140 Shattuck Ave. #2406, Berkeley, CA 94704. Order from the publisher.

"Training the Companion Dog," from Dr. Dunbar's British TV Series, James & Kenneth Publishers. (See address above).

The American Kennel Club produces videos on every breed of dog, as well as on hunting tests, field trials and other areas of interest to purebred dog owners. For more information, write to AKC/Video Fulfillment, 5580 Centerview Dr., Suite 200, Raleigh, NC 27606.

chapter 13

Resources

Breed Clubs

Every breed recognized by the American Kennel Club has a national (parent) club. National clubs are a great source of information on your breed. You can get the name of the secretary of the club by contacting:

The American Kennel Club
51 Madison Avenue
New York, NY 10010
(212) 696-8200

There are also numerous all-breed, individual breed, obedience, hunting and other special-interest dog clubs across the country. The American Kennel Club can provide you with a geographical list of clubs to find ones in your area. Contact them at the above address.

Registry Organizations

Registry organizations register purebred dogs. The American Kennel Club is the oldest and largest in this country, and currently recognizes over 130 breeds. The United Kennel Club registers some breeds the AKC doesn't (including the American Pit Bull Terrier and the Miniature Fox Terrier) as well as many of the same breeds. The others included here are for your reference; the AKC can provide you with a list of foreign registries.

American Kennel Club
51 Madison Avenue
New York, NY 10010

United Kennel Club (UKC)
100 E. Kilgore Road
Kalamazoo, MI 49001-5598

American Dog Breeders Assn.
P.O. Box 1771
Salt Lake City, UT 84110
(Registers American Pit Bull Terriers)

Canadian Kennel Club
89 Skyway Avenue
Etobicoke, Ontario
Canada M9W 6R4

National Stock Dog Registry
P.O. Box 402
Butler, IN 46721
(Registers working stock dogs)

Orthopedic Foundation for Animals (OFA)
2300 E. Nifong Blvd.
Columbia, MO 65201-3856
(Hip registry)

Activity Clubs

Write to these organizations for information on the
activities they sponsor.

American Kennel Club
51 Madison Avenue
New York, NY 10010
(Conformation Shows, Obedience Trials, Field
Trials and Hunting Tests, Agility, Canine Good

Citizen, Lure Coursing, Herding, Tracking,
Earthdog Tests, Coonhunting.)

United Kennel Club
100 E. Kilgore Road
Kalamazoo, MI 49001-5598
(Conformation Shows, Obedience Trials, Agility,
Hunting for Various Breeds, Terrier Trials and
more.)

North American Flyball Assn.
1342 Jeff St.
Ypsilanti, MI 48198

International Sled Dog Racing Assn.
P.O. Box 446
Norman, ID 83848-0446

North American Working Dog Assn., Inc.
Southeast Kreisgruppe
P.O. Box 833
Brunswick, GA 31521

Trainers

Association of Pet Dog Trainers
P.O. Box 385
Davis, CA 95617
(800) PET–DOGS

American Dog Trainers' Network
161 West 4th St.
New York, NY 10014
(212) 727–7257

**National Association of Dog Obedience
Instructors**
2286 East Steel Rd.
St. Johns, MI 48879

Associations

American Dog Owners Assn.
1654 Columbia Tpk.
Castleton, NY 12033
(Combats anti-dog legislation)

Delta Society
P.O. Box 1080
Renton, WA 98057-1080
(Promotes the human/animal bond through
pet-assisted therapy and other programs)

Dog Writers Assn. of America (DWAA)
Sally Cooper, Secy.
222 Woodchuck Ln.
Harwinton, CT 06791

National Assn. for Search and Rescue (NASAR)
P.O. Box 3709
Fairfax, VA 22038

Therapy Dogs International
6 Hilltop Road
Mendham, NJ 07945